Pop Your
PATTERNS

THE NO-NONSENSE WAY TO CHANGE YOUR LIFE

SETH C. KADISH PSY.D.

WITH BROOKES NOHLGREN

Dedication

To the memory of my parents, Lois and Henry,
and to the daily presence of my wife, Sochi

Contents

Acknowledgments

To Denise, Glen and the staff and
clients of Milestones Ranch Malibu,
and to Brookes for helping me make it happen

Foreword

The subject of negative patterns of human thought, emotion and behavior is quite extensive and fascinating. Volumes upon volumes can be, and have been, written about this topic.

In this work, I attempted to set forth its most important elements, utilizing the knowledge and expertise gained from years of clinical experience in group homes, treatment centers, private practice, and prison. In addition, I used simple-to-read and easy-to-understand language, seasoned with jokes, stories and anecdotes when possible, with the intention of creating a fun and compelling experience for the reader.

"Pop Your Patterns" is intended to be the first step for the person interested in starting a journey of personal transformation. As the saying goes, "A journey of a thousand miles begins with a single step."

Let the journey begin.

Preface

I didn't set out to become an expert in helping people "pop" their negative patterns. Like many good things in my life, it happened by accident - or at least what seemed like an accident at the time. I was working as a case manager at a girls' group home just outside of Los Angeles. My clients were primarily Probation youth, sent to our facility by a judge on charges of drug use, gang activity, prostitution, or assaultive behavior. I had been assigned a new client, Lakeisha, a 15-year-old with big, expressive eyes. She was very pretty...but her attitude wasn't. Her nasty demeanor overshadowed her natural good looks.

Prior to Lakeisha, I'd tended to be soft-spoken and non-confrontational with new clients - exactly the way my counseling training had taught me to be. I was a model therapist, loving and warm. But I was becoming frustrated with my work. Without realizing it, I was tiptoeing around my clients. And I was starting to get the nagging feeling that I wasn't being as effective as I could, and ought to, be. In becoming a counselor, I wanted to make a powerful difference in people's lives. Now, fortunately, the breakthrough I needed was coming through my door.

When Lakeisha walked into the room and verbally attacked me, my years of training flew out the window. My natural instincts took over, and I reacted. As she pushed, I pushed right back.

"I don't want to be here!" she yelled. "I hate therapists, and this is bullshit! I ain't talkin' to you."

"Good. I don't want to talk to you. You're rude," I snapped back.

"Say what?" she said.

"Yeah, you heard me. You come into my office, you disrespect me. Why should I want to talk to you? In fact, get out!"

Lakeisha might not have been expecting my response, but I was only a little surprised. Truth be told, I'd never felt all that comfortable with the soft clinical style I had been trained in, one based on the 1950s work of the innovative therapist Carl Rogers, renowned for his mild and nondirective approach with clients. Though his method was highly respected, it just wasn't me.

I'm from Brooklyn, a pretty earthy place. And growing up there in the '60s and '70s, my friends and I were rooted in our parents' and grandparents' old-school ways of talking and acting. To give you an idea of what I mean, when I moved to California in 1986 and coworkers asked me what being from Brooklyn was like, I described it like this: "You guys had Student Government, cheerleaders, Honor Society, the school play. We had the Junior Witness Protection Program."

A few years ago my good friend Big Mike and I were reminiscing about how many of the kids we knew had died or been arrested back in the day - shot in the face during a cocaine deal, caught holding up a bank, murdered over drugs, leapt from a tall building in an LSD-induced suicide. Brooklyn was a rough place to grow up. Even my Little League coach got arrested for armed robbery! I used to joke that I should have known something was wrong when he'd tell me to steal second base...and sell it to the other team.

Though my neighborhood was fairly safe - with mostly Jews and Italians and a smattering of Irish, German, black, and Puerto Rican (safe, in part, because it was a Mob neighborhood) - there were dangers, to be sure, and I developed street smarts at an early age. My elementary school was in the bad part of town, near the housing projects, and my classmates were mostly tough, lower-class kids. All in all I liked them and they accepted me, but I always paid the proper attention to my surroundings and read people for who they were, sizing them up quickly to determine their mood and mindset. Early in life I developed the ability to spot people's "patterns" - the thoughts, emotions, and behavior that made up their reactions to the world. It was a matter of safety and survival.

The communication style in Brooklyn was a little rough too. *Blunt* is probably the best word for it, like the Brooklyn guy whose wife walked into the house after work and saw him sitting on the couch.

"Hi, honey," she said, "how was your day?"

"Fine," he replied. "Your cat is dead."

The woman was appalled at her husband's brusque statement.

"I can't believe you," she cried. "What terrible news! And did you have to say it like that?"

"Like what?"

"You could have said, 'Honey, I was home today and I left the window open. The cat got out, climbed up the drainpipe and went onto the roof. Then a sudden gust of wind came along and, honey, I'm so, so sorry, but your beloved Frisky is no longer with us.' You could have said it like that!"

The next day the wife walked into the house and saw her husband sitting on the couch.

"Hi, honey," she said, "how was your day?"

"Fine," he said. "I left the window open and your mother got out."

Brooklyn. Old school. It's where I come from, who I was raised to be.

My mother, too, instilled in me a "flair" for directness. Let's just say she was not your typical Jewish mother. "Sweet" is not a word I would use to describe her. Yet she was strong and compassionate. Most of all, she told it like it was. I'll never forget my sister's story about the time she took Mom to the funeral of one of her best friends. As the casket was being lowered into the ground, with the 200-some attendees silently looking on, my mom, in a loud sing-songy voice, said, "The End." My sister was mortified! But that's the way Mom was. She didn't mean anything cruel by it; it was just her (very blunt) way of admitting the truth, "He's gone."

The Brooklyn approach to life is real and it's raw; it's about accepting what is and dealing with life from that place. We cut right to the chase, got right to the point. And though my friends, family, and neighbors were often crass in their bluntness, there was something to be said about their straight and honest talk. Now, in my first meeting with Lakeisha, I was stumbling into my discovery of how this no-nonsense style could be helpful in a therapy setting.

Lakeisha sat on the couch, dumbfounded, more surprised than angry at my unusual reply.

"You want to hear how I see you?" I asked.

"Yeah," she said, "all right."

"Okay. Here goes. You're nasty and angry. You have a crappy attitude. But maybe you're hurt. Someone hurt or upset you and you go around dumping your anger onto other people, like me."

Lakeisha stared at me with her big eyes.

"I'm right, huh?" I said.

"A hundred percent," she said, a grin breaking out across her face.

Lakeisha's smile taught me in seconds what I've confirmed hundreds of times since - *people like to hear the truth*. The truth gets us grounded. It gives us a surge of power. Many of us spend a lot of time running from it, thinking that it'll run us over, but it doesn't. The truth doesn't kill. In fact, at the end of the day, it actually gives us an opportunity to discover how lovable and worthy we really are.

When I think back to my days as a kid in Brooklyn, I see that making fun of each other helped us in some ways because it kept us from indulging in too much shame. With all of us constantly teasing one another, we couldn't be so set in our defenses. We would hear the truth - and, don't get me wrong, it hurt - but then we would get over it and become less sensitive about our own shortcomings.

Keeping secrets, trying to conceal our shortcomings, creates the opposite effect. When we are protecting ourselves by hiding something we don't want others to know, it becomes impossible to accept our own imperfections and mistakes and to really be ourselves. Secrets stifle us; they warp us from the inside out. We get so fixated with covering them up that we become more and more afraid of looking at them, let alone embracing and dealing with them. This is why looking honestly in the mirror is so powerfully transformative in overcoming issues. The truth really does set us free.

With Lakeisha, my calling her on her negative pattern did a couple of things. It stopped her thoughts, feelings, and behavior in their tracks, it instantly brought the conversation into reality where we could address the pattern, it forged a connection between us, and she became open to insight. The doors flew open to talk about how her negativity was not helping her get what she really wanted in life - how, in fact, it was doing the opposite. We were also able to look at where and why her pattern had developed, and what purpose it had originally served. She was then freer to make a different choice that might be more aligned with her creating what would ultimately make her happy.

From that point on as we worked together, Lakeisha began taking more responsibility for the way she was operating in the world, and I started using my new straightforward approach with all of my therapy clients. I continued to work with Probation youth, then later with maximum security inmates within the California Prison System, and eventually counseled dual diagnosis clients (people who suffer from coexisting psychiatric and chemical dependency issues) at several treatment centers in the Los Angeles area.

As it evolved, I came to call my approach Pattern Identification and Reduction Therapy™ or less formally, "Pointing Out Patterns" or "P.O.P." I help people "pop" their negative patterns. Time and again I have seen with my own eyes just how effective accurately reading people combined with a little compassionate truth-telling is. It always wins the day, creating breakthroughs with people from every walk of life. If this method can help inmates and drug abusers - people whose negative patterns are so deeply ingrained that they have acted out in the most extremes of destructive behavior - to lead happier, more fulfilling lives, it can work for you too. That is my purpose in writing this book and my sincere wish for you.

PROLOGUE:
You CAN Change

There's a single concept I need you to embrace if this method is going to work for you. And that is that *change is possible*, even for you. I don't care if you've been doing something the same way your entire life - you *can* change. I can say this with absolute certainty because I've done it myself, and I've helped many others do it too. And I'm not just talking about easy changes. I'm referring to changing the things about yourself that are so deeply engrained they may feel like *who you are*. Things that, once changed, will make a dramatic difference in how you relate to the world and how you experience your life.

How I Changed

I'll start with my own example. When I was 26 years old I "popped" my pattern of violence. My excessive anger had been coloring all of my relationships: with my dad, my girlfriends, even at work. I'd always been a scrappy kid, and I'd had my share of schoolyard fights. I was very aggressive on the ball court, too. When I was six years old, in a junior basketball league on a team coached by my dad, the kid I was defending went up for a layup. I couldn't stop him. He went UP - and I pulled his pants DOWN. Aggressive, huh?

At age 26, I was in a sketch comedy troupe with my best friend, Big Mike, and a few other folks. We performed in several Manhattan clubs. At one of the rehearsals, I became angry with a guy in the group. I was also studying martial arts at the time and was pretty good. I knew how to hit hard and was working toward my brown belt. Instead of smashing him in the face, I smashed my hand against the wall in his East Village apartment.

This was nothing new for me. I had been putting my hands through walls for years. The basement in my childhood home was a minefield of holes that I'd cover up with posters of rock stars. Well, I hit my hand against this guy's wall - which turned out to be made of concrete. I remember saying, "Ouch!" shaking it, and ignoring it for a few days. The fist swelled and I finally went to the doctor, who told me I'd broken my knuckle. The doctor put me in a cast for a few months. When Big Mike saw it, he was very sympathetic. "Hey, *shmuck*," he laughed, "maybe you'll stop punching walls."

Well, I decided I *would* stop punching walls. And, more importantly, I took it a step further…

But let me go back in time for a minute to when I was 17 and working as a waiter in a crummy hotel in the mountains of New Jersey. It was the middle of the summer and I decided to quit the job. I called Big Mike and our buddy the Bean to come get me and take me back to Brooklyn. They were en route when I went into the owner's office to give my notice. His nephew, the maitre d', was a young guy, maybe 25 at the time, probably 6'0" and 170 lbs. I was smaller then, and he had a couple of inches on me, plus 30 lbs.

As I told the owner I was leaving, the maitre d' threw a punch at me when I wasn't looking and clipped me in the jaw. He wore a ring, which left a nasty gash across my cheek. I jumped on him and we tussled in the lobby of the fourth-rate hotel, sending old ladies and kids scurrying for cover. Big Mike and the Bean arrived, coincidentally, a few moments later, and it so happened that they had brought Crazy Kenny with them. Mike had been a lineman on the high school football team, the Bean stood 6'2" (though skinny), and Ken was also over six feet tall and brawny. They wanted to tear the maitre d' from limb to limb. I said no.

"Why not?"

I knew that the hotel owner was good friends with the local sheriff.

"Because it's not worth it. You guys will throw him a beating, and you'll end up in jail."

Jump forward to age 26. My hand had healed, and I continued to study martial arts. After workouts at the dojo in Manhattan, I'd ride the train home to Brooklyn with my gym bag in hand, pumped and alert.

Now, I'd heard rumors that the maitre d' who'd once cold-cocked me was living in my low-rent neighborhood - a far cry from his nice New Jersey suburb. He'd married a local girl and was supposedly living in a basement apartment somewhere near me. I had forgotten all about this, that is, until I walked through a subway car and saw the guy sitting in a corner. Now in his mid-30s, he was prematurely graying, staring at the floor, with two large shopping bags by his side. He looked like a hen-pecked husband - a loser, a sad sack.

I moved closer and closer, like a gunfighter in a western. I felt my heart beating. I was *ready*. I continued to get closer, but he never looked up. As I got near him, I stared down at him for a second. He still didn't look up. You know what I did?

Nothing.

It's a moment I'll forever be proud of. I could have easily demolished this guy in a fight. I could have had my revenge. But I chose not to.

My sensei had cautioned us repeatedly to use our martial arts knowledge only in self-defense. But it was more than that. I didn't want revenge, I didn't want bloodshed. I wanted to feel *powerful*. And walking away from the maitre d' gave me a sense of power.

My propensity to violence broke, just like that. I didn't know the concept of popping patterns back then, but I'd popped one, sure enough. My anger and violence diminished radically because of that event and the fist-in-the-wall, as did the way I viewed the world. My thoughts and self-talk had changed too. Instead of, "I'm weak and I have to fight," it was, "I feel strong and I don't have to fight at all."

I can't tell you how much this improved my life. The anger and violence I once experienced so frequently, that had been creating turbulence in most areas of my life, lifted. Instantly, I became freer and lighter. When my anger did flare up again at times, I was able to control it - rather than it controlling me.

So, as you probably guessed by now, I'm all for change. I've felt the freedom it can give, and I believe in it fervently. Call it "transformation," "conversion," "makeover," what have you - I believe in it. And I believe we *all* can change.

The Mechanics of Change

But how do we change? What are the mechanics? This book will take you through it, step by step. But first let's look at another example, this time a classic. Ever think about what makes a classic a classic? It's that it resonates deep within us a truth about being human. Charles Dickens's *A Christmas Carol* is such a story. It's the quintessential tale of a man who transforms his negative patterns. Scrooge's metamorphosis strikes such a chord in our collective psyche that Hollywood has resurrected the story numerous times, including several dramatic movie versions, a musical, and even a comedy starring Bill Murray.

Here's the plot, in case you don't know it. In 18th-century London, Ebenezer Scrooge is a cold-hearted, miserly, and dour businessman. He is distant and foreboding, and filled with mistrust. He dislikes people and despises anything that relates to joy or happiness. "Bah, humbug!" is his infamous refrain to anyone who dares wish him a "Merry Christmas."

The story unfolds on Christmas Eve, as Scrooge is visited by three ghosts who come to show him scenes from his despicable life - past, present, and future. He has no choice but to accompany them on this journey through time, and he is forever changed by what he sees. For the first time in his life, he has the ability to observe his patterns and see himself as he really is. He reacts with horror, sadness, and regret. But the story doesn't end there. Scrooge is also given *hope* - that if he changes his thinking and behavior (in other words, changes his patterns), the dreadful future he has been shown will not come to pass. He can still change the course of his fate.

Like so many of us, before a mirror was forced upon him, Scrooge had no interest in seeing himself honestly. Yet it is only through self-reflection that we can change. Scrooge's transformation is motivated by sadness over the harm he has inflicted on others and by regret over a wasted life, the fear of a painful future, and the hope for something better. He feels both a *need* and a *desire* to change, so that he may connect with others and bring about joy and happiness for them as well as for himself. He follows through with this new commitment by making new and different choices, demonstrated by the kindness and gifts he gives to others on Christmas Day.

All change requires certain key ingredients. The first is *wanting* to change, seeing a *need* to change. *Motivation* is a must! This is followed closely by *believing* that change is possible. Not everyone does believe it, and often it's the feeling of helplessness or hopelessness that keeps a person stuck in a dysfunctional pattern. And the final ingredient is *commitment*. Thinking about change is not enough. You will have to do the *actions* that bring change about. This book will help you do that.

Believing You Can Change

Do you believe you can confront your negative patterns? Do you believe you can change?

For several years, I conducted a weekly prison group around popping patterns. We looked at participants' errors in thinking, their issues, emotions, and behavior. A typical cohort consisted of several murderers, a few armed robbers, third-strikers, drug dealers, and the occasional arsonist or contract killer.

Do you think inmates, stuck in the routine and confines of a prison environment, want to change their patterns? You bet they do! Like all human beings, they want to learn and grow, to be free of pain and unhappiness. Just like you and me, they want social connection, hope, and a sense of control. It's true that change is difficult for them, but some manage to do it. And if *they* can change - living in the pressure cooker of a maximum prison yard where stabbings, rapes, drug deals, and gangs are a daily threat - where one wrong word or small sign of disrespect can get a person hurt or killed - if they can make changes amid this constant barrage of challenges, then *you* can change too.

Inmate Jamison was a tall, lanky man with long hair and glasses. He was quite intelligent and enjoyed coming to groups and talking to me one-on-one. Prior to coming to prison, he had been a pharmacist's assistant at a nearby hospital. Ordinarily mild-mannered, Jamison had been stealing various drugs from his workplace, and also bingeing on methamphetamine for days and days.

One night, he had an argument with two guys over a parking space. Jamison, paranoid and agitated, took a butcher knife out of his boot and stabbed the first guy in the heart in front of a crowd of people. The second guy, panic-stricken, attempted to run away. Jamison hunted him down and stabbed him to death, seconds before the cops could arrive and arrest him.

In prison, despite the violence in his past - or perhaps because of it - Jamison wanted desperately to change. He wanted to be less violent, more forgiving, and less quick to fly into a rage. We made a pact: if he felt like "going off" on somebody, he'd come talk to me first.

Sure enough, a week later Jamison wanted to seek revenge on a correctional officer, who he felt was picking on him. I dropped everything I was doing (I had an enormous line of guys to see that day) and met with Jamison in a small, makeshift office complete with two man-sized cages used to house difficult inmates.

"Doc, what do I do?" he asked.

"Do nothing, Jamison. Or, rather, do what you don't usually do - let it go."

"But that bastard - "

"Nope. Stop right there. You're gonna justify hurting the guy."

"He's lucky you're here, Dr. K."

"I'm glad I am, Jamison."

Jamison did not attack the guard. As it turned out, he had given up the habit of attacking guards. He had popped his pattern, learning to walk away from confrontation, unless it involved a direct physical threat.

I saw Jamison a while later, strolling on the yard.

"Kadish!" he shouted, coming over to me and touching knuckles through the fence. "How are you?"

"Good, man. How's your temper?"

"Cool."

"Glad to hear it, Jamison."

"And I finally feel ready for a relationship."

"What's her name?"

"Eddie in Three Building."

But that's another story.

The Support You Need

The book you are holding in your hands is dedicated to helping you transform the patterns that are ruining your life - the ones that are killing your relationships and causing you to miss opportunities for greater joy and growth. It will teach you how to confront yourself in the mirror - owning your negative thoughts, feelings, and behaviors - and will give you the tools you need to choose more positive ways of responding to life that will build your self-esteem and allow you to get what you truly want.

One quick clarification, though. Popping negative patterns doesn't have to be harsh. Unlike the ghosts' approach with Scrooge, I'm not going to *scare* you into changing. It simply isn't necessary. My method is quite different. You see, changing our negative patterns is actually easier if, before focusing on what's wrong with us -what desperately needs to change - we first take an honest assessment of what's working well, what's positive about us - our strengths and past successes - and build on those. Now that doesn't sound too bad, does it?

If you're like many of my clients, at this point you may be whining, "But I don't have any strengths or successes. I'm a loser!" And I'll reply in fine Brooklyn manner, "Why are you *lying* to me?" If you think you have no strengths or experiences of success, you are lying to yourself and to me.

This is important to recognize because, as we go through life, we paint a picture of everything we are and everything we do. If you think your life is only made of negatives, you are seeing only part of your picture. The POP approach is all about truth-telling and looking in the mirror, and that must include seeing positive patterns too. Drawing on our positives helps us work through our negatives. So you're just going to have to trust me here and give this idea a shot. Let's take a look.

Take a moment and think back over your life and to something you did well - anything you ever did right - and write it down. This can be *anything*. I don't care what it is, just write it down. It might be a good grade on a test or quiz, a kind or encouraging word you gave to someone, a poem or story you wrote. There will be thousands and thousands of little and big things that you have done in your lifetime that show your intelligence, compassion, artistry, competence, and many other positive qualities and attributes. Write some of them down now.

Next I want you to think specifically about how you have changed during your lifetime. "Transform" means to "change form." Think about areas of growth, advancement, evolution, maturing, or just switching direction from the one you were going in. List some of the changes you have made or times you did something different from what you were doing before.

Viewing the whole picture of your life, the good and the bad, will determine the way you see yourself, and what you tell yourself will often determine how you perform. If all we see about ourselves is bad, and all we say is negative, then we won't be able to perform well to make positive change. It just won't happen. Change requires courage, and *encouragement* is the fastest way to develop it! That's because we are who we say we are. Therefore, having a healthy sense of our strengths and speaking to ourselves in encouraging terms is a crucial part of achieving any success.

In looking at the lists you created, can you see that you do, in fact, have at least some propensity to change? As I said before, we *all* do. I've seen it time and time again. I've seen it in inmates, in people with drug addictions, and in everyday people. And I know you can do it too.

In order to change, you need to be committed to it. At this point, I'm not asking for a full-blown commitment to change, only that you be open to the *possibility* that you *can* change. If you agree that that's a possibility, and you're willing to give yourself permission to look at yourself honestly in an attempt to change, and you feel ready to go for it, then turn this page and launch into the book.

If you're not ready, that's okay too. You always have the right to say no. In fact, in my work with clients, I welcome "No." What I do not accept is "maybe," "whatever," "sure," or "I'll think about it." Either you want to take a step forward, which is an act of courage, or you don't. Either choice is okay. If you're not quite ready, just put the book down and come back to it when you've truly had enough of your patterns. Often, we need to get totally exhausted by our patterns before we see the need to change them. Or, if you feel that this approach just isn't for you, chuck the book altogether or sell it on eBay. The choice is always yours, and anything you choose is okay with me.

This book *is* for you if you want a simple guide on how to change your life. It's for you if your life is currently unmanageable, a mess, a disaster and you'd like that to change. It's *not* for you if you think a mere book will cure your problems. It won't. It will get the ball rolling, but a major and instantaneous change won't occur just by reading. Change takes practice.

However, I can promise you this. This book will point you strongly in the right direction. It will get you looking at yourself, which is the starting point for all change, and it will offer you activities and techniques that, when applied consistently, will lead to true, lasting, positive change. Want to join me in the journey? Great, just turn the page...

PART I
UNDERSTANDING
YOUR PATTERNS

CHAPTER ONE:
What Are Patterns and Why Would You Want to "Pop" Them?

A pattern, by definition, is something that occurs over and over again. In this book, "pattern" refers to the reactions and responses we exhibit in our daily lives - in other words, the combination of our thoughts, emotions, and behaviors. It works something like this: (1) We experience something in the outer world, (2) we think something (often unconsciously) about that experience, (3) a feeling gets provoked by our own thought, and (4) then we take action in the physical world based on how we feel. These things may or may not happen in this exact order, as much of it occurs simultaneously.

Together these elements form a pattern. And like most habits or routines, we perform these patterns of thought, emotion, and behavior repeatedly, often not even aware that we're doing them. They are obsessive (thought) and compulsive (action) by nature. The neural pathways they have formed in our brain are grooved in, requiring real effort if we are to change them and create new pathways.

Patterns, like any other habit, can be positive or negative. By "positive" I'm referring to the ones that benefit us and bring about true happiness, the ones that help us get what we want in life - the beliefs, attitudes, habits, and responses that allow us to connect with other people, take care of ourselves, and go for our goals in a confident and productive way. Perseverance, altruism, kindness, and independence are examples of positive patterns. (Note, however, that I did not include innate qualities such as intelligence, artistry, or physical ability. Innate talents are God-given, in our genes. Positive patterns are acquired behaviors that we develop through effort.)

Negative patterns, then, are those combined thoughts, emotions, and behaviors that limit us or create havoc in our lives, destroying what brings us happiness and preventing us from getting what we really want. If you've ever heard someone say, "He's his own worst enemy," it was the person's negative patterns the comment was referring to. Blame, self-pity, justification, attack, defense, anxiety, depression, intimidation, and seduction are but a few common negative patterns.

To be clear, this book will focus on negative patterns. From this point on, when you read the word "patterns," we're referring to negative and not positive patterns.

Let's look at an extreme but vivid illustration of negative patterns in action. In the films *The Godfather I* and *II*, Michael Corleone, played by Al Pacino, responds to his circumstances with manipulation, treachery, and intimidation. Though he thinks these tactics will help him protect his family, they eventually bring about the exact opposite result. Michael alienates his wife and kills his brother-in-law as well as his own brother. In order to save his family, he wipes many of them out. How's that for irony?

One of my clients, Liam, is an angry guy. He's constantly irritated, upset, and ready to fight the world. Now, I'm not saying that anger in and of itself is such an awful thing. It can help us stand up to injustices or let others know when they are crossing the boundaries of what is right for us. Anger becomes a problem, though, when it dominates our lives. It can result in failed relationships or self-destructive habits such as drug abuse. In Liam's case, his constant anger constitutes a negative pattern because it causes him to lose jobs, girlfriends, and roommates, and to alienate family members. His anger is an unwarranted response to many situations in his life ˙ and it has thrown his life out of balance.

Rebelliousness is another common pattern. Like anger, being a rebel is not necessarily a bad thing. *Mature* rebels - George Washington, Mohandas Gandhi, Jesus Christ, to name a few - understand what they are fighting for and why. But I know a lot more of the *immature* kind of rebel - they fill our prisons and treatment centers. They shoot dope, disrespect others, and are angry at everything. You can tell me all day long how wonderful and passionate they are, but I'll counter that they're adolescent and stuck in an endless cycle of meaningless defiance. The immature rebel is merely angry and self-pitying. He's often young or, at the very least, his thinking is juvenile.

One such character is Randall McMurphy, in the film *One Flew Over the Cuckoo's Nest*. Now you may argue that McMurphy is rebelling against a system that grinds him and everyone else down, but I will refute that he is unrealistic and wasting his time. I get the inspirational part, and I love him for it. But if he were my client, I'd probably say, "Man, if you really want to change the system, get a law degree." Immature rebels, like James Dean in *Rebel Without a Cause*, don't change anything. They tug at our hearts with their bravery and courage, but ultimately their gestures are rooted in anger and frustration and their battles are fought for themselves, not for others.

History and fiction are teeming with figures who display negative thinking, poor emotional impulse control, and destructive behavior. Batman is depressive, angry, and troubled. King David is filled with guilt after having Bathsheba's husband killed to get his hands on her. And Samson lets Delilah sweet-talk him into cutting his hair - talk about a people-pleaser! I think you could go so far as to say that every popular story has, at its heart, a protagonist with a negative pattern. This is because storytelling is an age-old, human way of attempting to understand ourselves and make sense of our lives. The most meaningful and inspiring stories are the ones that accurately portray our shortcomings and struggles - that speak honestly about the human condition. Stories, including films, can be very helpful at showing us our patterns as well as our ability to rise above them.

Like our favorite film characters, we all have patterns, both mild and extreme, that create our unhappiness and suffering. This is the human condition. And as you will learn in Chapter 2, our patterns are not some cosmic joke being played at our expense. Rather, they are the result of the evolution of our species, designed specifically for our safety and survival here on planet Earth. They form during childhood to protect us from both real and perceived threats to our physical or emotional well-being. The problem, as we shall see, is that what is useful to us in childhood can become toxic to us as adults.

Negative Patterns vs. Mental Disorders

Now that we have defined and illustrated negative patterns, a quick distinction should be made between a negative pattern and a true *mental disorder*, such as schizophrenia. A schizophrenic sees and hears things that aren't there, suffers from false or weird beliefs and bizarre thinking. A sad and common example is the unwashed guy pushing a shopping cart down the street, yelling at imaginary demons.

The schizophrenic needs medications in order to have a semblance of a normal life. That doesn't mean that he doesn't also suffer from negative thinking, emotions, and behavior. It does mean that he's got to deal with his hallucinations and delusions before working on his negative patterns (assuming his clinician thinks this is at all a viable idea).

If you know that you suffer from a psychiatric disorder, keep that in mind while reading this book. For instance, if you are very depressed or have a bipolar disorder, consult with a doctor. He will more than likely insist that you take appropriate medications. Or if you're not sure about the state of your mental health, go to a licensed mental health clinician immediately and have yourself checked out. I work with many people diagnosed with bipolar, depressive, and anxiety disorders, as well as what we call personality disorders, such as borderline, antisocial, and histrionic, but I can help them only if they are medically stable.

Unlike a psychiatric disorder, a negative pattern is not primarily associated with chemical imbalances or brain injuries. It is a way of thinking about and acting in the world, and as such has to do with thoughts, emotions, attitudes, and behaviors.

Can a person have a psychiatric disorder and a negative pattern? Yes. As I said, a schizophrenic can still have negative patterns. Extremely depressed and anxious people are almost always affected by negative patterns. But to reiterate, the physiological must be addressed before the negative pattern can be tackled.

Reasons to Change

Negative patterns can cause us grief in many ways. You don't have to look far to see how true this is. As a former staff psychologist at the California State Prison-Los Angeles County and current counselor to high-end dual diagnosis clients, I have worked with some of the most despised and neglected men in society as well as some of the most well-to-do and privileged - all in the same week! These facilities are filled with people whose negative patterns have gotten the best of them, and one of the great lessons I've learned in my work with these two opposite populations is that human beings are truly no different from one another. We all are essentially the same.

But *what* is the same within all of us? Our thoughts, emotions, and behaviors. In other words, our *patterns*. The outer packaging may look quite different, but rest assured, in essence we are alike. The successful businessman with relationship troubles is much more like the murderer serving a life sentence than he will ever know. You might think otherwise, but I have treated both guys in the same week, and their patterns can be strikingly similar. I know - because I've got the same patterns, too. The difference is often just a matter of degree. *Individuals are unique, but patterns are universal.*

I used to teach a class on "The Criminal Mind." The graduate students would eagerly anticipate learning the secrets of the criminal mind. It's got to be a gene, or a specific part of the brain, right?

Sorry to disappoint, but what I see as the criminal mind is usually *immaturity*. Yep, that's it. The whole secret. People think of criminals as thugs, and yet I know many who are bright, intelligent, and sensitive. You say, "They must be cold, heartless, and sociopathic." It's true - some are. But many are capable of fear, empathy, loyalty, honor, and warmth. So why then do they choose the criminal path? Because they are *impulsive* and *reactive*. Their thinking is at best adolescent, at worst infantile. Many never learned to think at all; they simply bought into a negative belief system about themselves and the world at large. Plenty of gangsters I know have gone down that antisocial road and lived to regret it.

Remember the little girl in *Willie Wonka and the Chocolate Factory* who wanted the Oompa-Loompa, and wanted it NOW? That's the thinking of the criminal who walks into your house with a shotgun at 3:00 a.m. and wants some cash NOW. The entitled little girl and demanding criminal share the same thinking. If she had a shotgun, she'd walk into your house at 3:00 a.m. and take all the Oompa-Loompas she wanted, trust me.

Again, we *all* have these patterns. It's simply a question of degree. Do you think you're so radically different from the criminal? Maybe. *But maybe not.* Take a look at yourself. Are you ever demanding? Threatening? Impulsive? Reactive?

I see demanding people all the time, none of whom are criminals. In the restaurant angrily telling the waiter, "I'm in a hurry. I need that martini NOW!" In the supermarket, rushing through the aisles, like they're in the Daytona Grocery 500. At the car wash, berating some poor worker about a water spot on the hood, a speck of dust on the fender.

You want to see threatening and potentially violent behavior? Try parking at the health food store in my neighborhood. The lot is tiny, and the drivers have difficulty maneuvering into the tight spots. They are impatient, challenging, and ready to blow up at a moment's notice. The kicker? Half of them are 75-year-old ladies with blue hair.

My point, of course, is not that the majority of us are on par with the criminal about to steal our stuff, but that we share similar patterns of thought, emotion, and behavior and that often the difference is only a question of extremes. I also want you to see that you don't need to face jail time or threats to your physical survival to experience the harmful effects of your patterns or to have the incentive to change them. If you're very lucky, your patterns are only having a minor impact on your life. If you're like most people, the impact is moderate to severe.

Ask yourself this: "Am I really *happy* with my life right now?" If no, why not? Another way to ask is, "Am I getting *what I want*?" People don't realize that it's actually in our self-interest to change our patterns. It's selfish, if you want to think of it that way. So many times, we think we are trying to change for the other people in our lives, for our spouse or children, but, really, the bottom line is that we do it for ourselves. You have to look in the mirror and be willing to see yourself making changes so that *you* can get what *you* want.

Here's an example. Laura was dumping anger on people where it wasn't warranted. It was not unusual for her to get upset and curse at several members of the rehab clinic's staff.

"What do you make of that?" I asked her immediately following her outburst.

"They deserved it," she huffed.

"So, you're blaming *them* for you dumping your crummy anger on them?" I asked calmly.

"Uh, it's not a big deal," she shrugged.

"Maybe it's not a big deal to *me*, and maybe not even to *them*, but I think it's a big deal to *you*," I said.

"No, it's cool," she said nonchalantly.

"Hold on, now," I said. "Where is that anger interfering with what you want in life?"

"Like what?" she asked.

"You tell me you want a boyfriend. How successful have you been at maintaining a relationship? You told me you were all washed up. How well are you doing with your family, your parents? You told me you were butting heads. If you're being honest with yourself, you'll see that your pattern is really causing you problems in getting what you want."

Many of us struggle in relationships. Either we find ourselves in a difficult relationship or we are lonely and wishing to be in a good relationship. What I've gathered from all of the couples therapy I've facilitated is that divorce is the result of a clash of negative patterns. Perhaps the wife is overly emotive, histrionic, or excessively anxious; the husband may be passive, avoidant, with repressed emotions. We may experience difficult relationships with our boss, friends, or family members. We feel anxious in front of others, fearful of criticism, and worried about the future. But first and foremost, we are unhappy in our relationship with ourselves. We beat ourselves up on a regular basis.

Sam is an example many of us can relate to. A 32-year-old, part-time waiter/part-time web designer and wannabe playwright, he was not happy with his life. He had a sense that he could be more. He was drinking too much, and sometimes stole painkillers from his friend's medicine cabinet. He liked the way they made him feel - happy, relaxed, no worries.

Sam was frustrated and angry at his waiter's job. He really wanted to be a playwright. He knew that writing plays usually didn't pay much money, but it was fun. At work Sam was irritable with the customers, his boss, and the kitchen chef, who was always growling at him. Sam fantasized about throwing his serving apron and black bowtie at the boss and storming out of the restaurant.

Sam got along well with his mother, who had always spoiled him a bit, but rarely talked to his father, who was usually critical. He felt that his father looked at him with an expression of, "I know you're gonna screw up again soon. You always do. You're a quitter and a loser."

He was perpetually angry at his father, but a bit intimidated by him, too. Dad was a successful attorney, and physically strong and fit. Sam wished he could relax around his dad, but he couldn't. He took a painkiller in his folks' bathroom during his last visit home, and it helped him get through dinner. That, and two glasses of wine.

To look at Sam, you wouldn't know that he is in the middle of an intense inner struggle. He lives in a nice apartment, has a cute girlfriend, and seems to have decent relationships with his family. Sam talks about the theatre and one day winning the Pulitzer prize. He has charm and ambition. He's likable. But inwardly he's a mess. In fact, he is on the road to substance addiction, and possibly a breakdown. Why?

Because Sam's negative patterns are preventing him from feeling comfortable with himself and others. He is a self-beater, anxious, insecure, excessively angry, frustrated, and disconnected. Do any of his patterns also belong to you?

Think about the problems you have in the various areas of your life. Some areas may have more than others, but most areas will have some problems. And what is the common denominator in all of these areas? It's you, of course! Or more accurately, it's your patterns. A negative pattern will rear its ugly head and create chaos in most of your endeavors.

Take Kenneth, for example, who was feeling suicidal. He's a middle aged guy, in the throes of divorce, monetary problems, and worries about his future. He's also angry and chock full of self-pity. He blames his wife for his troubles. "She's a bitch! She's taking all the money!" Kenneth feels terrible for himself, viewing himself as alone, abandoned, and weak. To regain a sense of power, he threatens to kill himself. "That'll get her attention, won't it?"

When he's not blaming his wife, Kenneth is blaming his business partner, his friends, and of course me, his therapist. What does he have to show for all the blame? Financial failure, a ruined marriage, and friends who run at the sight of him.

My point is this: I rarely encounter a client whose negative patterns show up in only one area of their life. Blamers blame constantly. Angry people get angry all the time. Deceivers lie to themselves and others.

The good news is that if you diminish, or eradicate, a negative pattern in one area of your life, other areas will improve too. Your whole life will improve. If seductive Marjorie stops seducing everyone she meets - and I'm not talking about just sexual seduction, but being coy and cute and inappropriately playful with bosses, coworkers, the guy at the supermarket - if she stops the seduction stuff, she won't be involved in weird romances that go nowhere, she'll gain the respect of her boss and coworkers (maybe even a promotion because she is quite a smart person), and people in other areas of her life will stop trying to use her and take advantage her. She doesn't see that *she* creates their desire to use her.

Just as one pattern leads to another, clearing up one pattern will lead to the diminishing or disappearance of other patterns.

Regaining Your Power

Another major benefit of eradicating our patterns is that we *regain our power*. I remember one day sitting down with one of my teen Probation girls - a feisty, hilarious, leader type of personality - and saying, "It's too bad you have no power." Oh, she got very indignant, but I wanted to rile her up a little bit.

"What do you mean? I have *a lot* of power!" she said.

"No, you have no power at all," I replied.

Then she insisted, "Yes I do!"

And I said, "You know what, I'm going to take your power away from you in 60 seconds."

"How are you going to do that?" she asked.

"I'm going to cause you to have an emotional reaction that you don't want to have, and you're going to feel powerless and out of control. I know how to make you angry in 60 seconds."

The impulsive, reactive nature of our patterns causes us to feel at the mercy of outside forces; we're emotionally chaotic, we lack self-control. Even if we don't feel out of control, there's still a nagging sense that something is wrong because inwardly we feel powerless, chaotic, turbulent, and that's because we haven't really worked through the patterns or the underlying emotional issues.

There once was a man who wanted to change his negative patterns, so he joined the local monastery. The only condition was that it was a silent retreat. The man was not allowed to say anything except for once every five years, when he was permitted to write two words on a small chalkboard.

Well, five silent years go by, and the guy is brought in front of the head monk and his assistant, who asks, "Is there anything you want to write?"

The guy vigorously nods his head and writes, "Food stinks."

Five more years go by, and the same ritual repeats: the head monk and his assistant ask him if there's anything he wants to write.

This time the guy writes, "Bed hard."

Another five years elapse, and the assistant asks, "Would you like to write anything?"

The guy nods yes, scrawls, "I quit," on the chalk-board, and with that, storms off.

The assistant is appalled and wants to run after him.

"No, no," says the head monk.

"But he mustn't," cries the assistant.

"Never mind, let him go. All he does is complain."

Now, for argument's sake, let's say you meet someone with good self-restraint and self-control, who's been introspective and worked at their patterns. You can say what you want to them and they may react with some level of upset, but they will come back fairly quickly and process through it: "Oh, this is a trigger of my dad being critical. You called me a jerk and said I was stupid and skinny and dumb. OK, I got it. I'm good." But if you don't have that ability to process - to absorb, digest, make sense of, or find meaning in your issues, trials, and tribulations - not only do you flare up but you remain in a state of upset for minutes, hours, days, weeks, or years. You hate that person in perpetuity and now you are victimizing yourself more and more as you indulge in a cycle of vengeance, forever seeking payback. You can't let it go, so you're stuck with it. If you don't want to be stuck with a pattern and the powerlessness it creates, you have to be willing to relinquish it. That requires admitting you have it and working your way through it.

I worked with a client who had been very success-ful in life but had a dark little secret - he was illiterate. He could read and write at about a second-grade level. When he came into the program, he angrily told us, "Do *not* make me read or write. Do not embarrass me in that way." We agreed. Then one afternoon, at the end of a group therapy session, this man's hand went up and he said, "I want to tell you all something." He proceeded to share his secret with the whole group. Their reac-tion was very supportive, and the burden of holding the secret was lifted. He empowered himself by telling on himself.

If you go to the truth, if you look at your stuff, you become powerful. When you hide it, you become pow-erless. It's a real paradox. With secrets, we think we're strong because we're hiding the shame and guilt and secret material, but it is only when we have very little or no shame that we become truly powerful. The really powerful people I know are impossible targets, because there's *nothing there to hit*.

As you will learn from our discussions in Chapter 2 about the origins of patterns, many develop out of the need to feel important or to regain a sense of power. Telling on yourself and breaking your patterns is a won-derful first step to regaining power. That's what this book is all about.

Which Patterns Are Yours?

We all have the seeds of negative patterns within us. It's not a question of can we think crummy thoughts or perpetrate crummy actions, but *which* are ours? Your task is to discover yours, and pop them.

Imagine walking into a party filled with balloons of every imaginable color: sky blue, pale violet, lemon yellow, snow white, mint green, and cherry red. You have to figure out which color is yours. Let's pretend it's chocolate brown. When I say go, you dash around the room with a pin in your hand, popping all of the chocolate brown balloons.

Good job! You've succeeded. In the next room are hundreds more balloons, and you have more brown balloons in that room. But that's only one pattern. You have others. When all of the brown balloons are gone in all of the rooms, you get to find your *next* color.

As Grandma used to say back in Brooklyn, "*Oy vey!*"

That's Life

Joking aside, isn't this just the way life is? It doesn't do a bit of good to complain about it. Working through patterns *is* the growth process. It's part and parcel of living, of being human. It may even be the primary purpose of life itself - to learn our lessons, overcome our limitations and adversities, develop character, deepen and evolve as people.

Do you know the difference between a heroic story and a tragic one? I'll give you a hint: it's not about how grand or tragic the events of the story are. And it's not about whether the protagonist lives or dies. It's about *inner transformation.* Will the protagonist transcend his personal limitations and become someone greater in the end than he was when the story began? In a heroic story, the answer is yes. The protagonist faces his fears, shortcomings, or weaknesses, works through them, and becomes freer and more powerful because of the experience. In a tragedy, the protagonist either never wakes up to the lesson or he chooses not to deal with it. He fails to transform.

Some folks say that "life is a school" and that whenever our emotional issues get provoked it simply means that "school is in session." We are here to learn and grow, to eradicate the negative and amp up the positive, to be the most authentic and honest we can be - and that's a real challenge. I ask people in my therapy groups: "What is the one battle or struggle on the planet?" The answer is: "The battle with the *self.*"

Buddha said it this way: "Life is suffering." A lot of people want to escape that, but that's not a productive

position to take. The way to get out of it is to go *through* it.
I often tell my clients, "I want you to be uncomfortable."
Looking at ourselves honestly and eradicating our negative patterns *should not be comfortable*. In fact, the worst
thing someone can say to me after a therapy group is, "Oh,
your group was very *nice*." I want to throw myself off
the balcony! If you tell me, "I cried, I puked, I hated you,
I loved it, I learned something, it was compelling," then
we're getting somewhere. Changing your life will require
you to be uncomfortable, to get outside of your ordinary
patterns. Discomfort is not the enemy - *it is the solution.*

Now, I realize that nobody *likes* to feel uncomfortable. If you think about what it means, it's about fear,
about anxiety: "I potentially could be attacked in some
way, I'm vulnerable, I'm out there." But in order to grow,
it's important to increase our tolerance for it. When
someone is willing to say, "I woke up this morning in a
terrible mood, I'm feeling pretty awful and I don't know
why, but that's where I am," I say, "Great, let's see what
that's about," and then we explore it. One thing I often
say is, "Let's go below." Once you get one thing figured
out, don't stop there: *Go below!* Challenge yourself and
keep digging, and you'll find something more.

We're too easy on ourselves too much of the time.
The only real problem with that is we don't end up where

we want to be. It's not that we should be mean or brutal with ourselves - I'm not advocating that either. What I am advocating, though, is being okay where you are, in the midst of your suffering or discomfort, knowing that it's for a positive end.

Of course we want to have joy and good feelings, but for the right reasons. Not the joy and good feeling of gaining power at another's expense, or from drinking a bottle of alcohol or doing a line of cocaine. Rather, the joy you get when you can say, "You know, I really struggled today and I didn't give in to my usual patterns. When I blew out the tire on my car, I didn't react the way I normally would. Instead of cursing and crying and screaming, I simply acknowledged how I felt and problem-solved and then got back into my day, and I feel pretty good about that." It's an authentic view of ourselves and an authentic dealing with our issues - based in reality.

So, if life really is a "school," and there is nothing we can do to change the "curriculum" - shouldn't we make it a little easier on ourselves by accepting what is and embracing the process? The best thing you can do is "commit to struggle." To say to yourself, "I'm going to commit to trying to get there, to going through the process, and all the rest is gravy. I'm going to show up and meet myself where I am and move forward the best I can."

I believe that very few of us get to the level of self-actualization, nirvana, enlightenment, or whatever else you choose to call that stage of being beyond patterns and character flaws. Perhaps a few make it - Jesus, Buddha, and the like - but the rest of us fall far short. Yet at least we can feel good about taking the journey towards such a lofty goal. This venture in and of itself is noble and worthwhile.

I used to tell some of the inmates I counseled, "Be noble." They would often say to me in return, "I can try to be noble, Dr. Seth, but it won't make any difference, because no one else is." My reply was always the same: "I don't care. *You* be noble. It'll make a difference to *you*."

It's like the story of the lady on the beach, where the tide has washed up all these starfish on the shore and they're dying because they need to be in the water. And she is picking them up, one by one, and throwing them back in. The beach is covered with them. A guy comes along and says, "Lady, there's a million starfish out here. You think what you're doing is going to make a difference?" She looks at the starfish she's holding in her hand and says, "It'll make a difference to this one."

Taking this noble and worthwhile journey is how we become the heroes in our own lives. It transforms us into the people we truly desire to be. To take the next step on your hero's journey, just keep reading…

CHAPTER TWO:
Befriending Our Patterns

At this point I hope you're beginning to get a little excited and maybe even asking: "What are *my* negative patterns, and how can I work through them?" The first step in eradicating negative patterns is identifying and understanding them, and realizing that they are, in a sense, your friend. This means discovering where they come from, when and how they developed, what purpose they've served, and why they are still lingering in your life. We will also look at where negative patterns most often show up and what the best mindset is for approaching the work needed to successfully overcome them.

Where Do Patterns Come From?

People often ask me, "Why do I have this pattern?" My answer is, "You have it for a sane and logical reason, because it was helpful to you once upon a time." The smaller picture about this "once upon a time" is that patterns develop in childhood as a response to our various life experiences. They arise for the purpose of protecting us physically and emotionally, from both real and perceived threats. We'll discuss this aspect of the development of patterns in just a moment. But first, let's look at the bigger picture of the formation of our patterns.

The Origin of Our Patterns - Human Evolution

I'm a big believer in evolutionary psychology. It all makes perfect sense to me - how today's dysfunctional responses like people-pleasing, guilt, aggression, and seduction have their roots in prehistoric times, in the brains of our ancestors who lived millions of years ago. These mechanisms have been handed down to us, from generation to generation, ever since. The drive behind our responses to life is part of our physiology - it's hard-wired in our brains.

If we look at ourselves from a purely physiological perspective, we'll see that our two main functions are 1) to survive and 2) to create more human beings. With a little investigation, we can see that all of our human thoughts, emotions, and behaviors revolve around these two aims: to live another day and to make babies (or at least care for them). It all makes sense when you consider the circumstances we as a species were dealing with when our brains and bodies developed.

Originally, we were hunter-gatherers. We lived in caves and made our living by hunting animals and picking fruits, nuts, and berries. We found that we were more effective at providing for ourselves when we performed in groups. Life at its simplest meant we worked as a team to hunt animals ("Hey, Joe, you go to the right, I'll run off to the left, and, Larry, you stand right there and let the woolly mammoth run right into you!"). In order to feed and protect ourselves, we *needed* the group. Depending on the group for both individual and species survival led to the development of a psychology that allowed for living and working together.

Our needs to survive and to produce offspring also meant that we had to guard against enemy tribesmen who wanted to take our food and/or our women. We needed those women to produce more of us (Ugs, Oobs, and Maks - personally, I think I was a Goog). But first we had to attract them to us, which meant that we had to offer them something. And the main thing they wanted was security - protection from the elements, animals, enemies - and to be fed and clothed. Their main job was to produce those kids, and they needed the best guys possible to do that.

So, what does all this have to do with negative patterns? Well, a lot!

Our basic emotions arose out of these early conditions to help ensure our survival and our ability to attract a mate and have babies. First let's look at our most primal emotions of anger and fear.

If we didn't have anger, how could we be hunters? How could we kill? Without the energy that anger provides, how could we chase after the beast or defend ourselves or stop the other guy from taking our woman? Physiologically, anger shuts down the digestive system, increases the heart beat, sends adrenaline coursing through the body, enabling us to go on the attack. Fight or flight. Anger was absolutely necessary for our survival.

As for fear, if we didn't have anxiety we might walk right off a cliff, waltz up to a saber-toothed tiger, or say, "My, isn't that a pretty little rattlesnake?" Anxiety was a mechanism for warning us of danger, for keeping us safe and, like anger, we needed a healthy amount of it to survive.

As we've noted, human beings were (and are) social animals. We had to get together and function as a group. We had to cooperate. But for this to happen, we needed certain rules for interacting with one another. We couldn't just do whatever we wanted, whenever we wanted. If we did that, there'd be no social order. We needed to be able to trust one another. If we violated trust, then, we just might get thrown out of the group, which could have some pretty bad consequences. An alligator, lion, bear, or cannibal was waiting around the mouth of the cave, hoping someone would get thrown out because it was just about dinnertime.

We needed the group and so we had to fit in. As a result, we developed an inner mechanism, in the form of guilt and shame, to prevent us from doing something that might get us thrown out. And, if we *did* do something against the code of the group, we learned to lie, deceive, and manipulate, to blame others, and to justify so that no one would be the wiser about us.

This need to protect our image leads to self-importance. Self-importance is synonymous with "ego" (at least the way the word is used in contemporary language; e.g., "That guy has a big ego."). You can call it vanity, if you prefer. It's pretty much the same thing. All of our negative patterns are rooted in our self-importance, our need to feel important. It boils down to this: when we feel our importance is being questioned or attacked, we become shamed, afraid, or enraged.

Where does self-importance come from? We need a little bit of it for survival purposes - to protect and care for ourselves. But our egos are like hungry monsters, quickly growing out of control. I believe self-importance comes about either 1) because people around us tell us we're special and pamper, kiss, and stroke us or 2) we feel undervalued and unappreciated, and so we puff ourselves up to look bigger and more spectacular.

We have evolved this way. Our self-importance is a defense against external threats, such as other people making fun of us. How does this relate to survival and procreation? If they disrespect or humiliate us, they may feel they can take it a step farther and do us real harm. Just ask any prisoner about this. In prison, you simply can't afford to let an insult go unanswered. As for procreation, if a woman sees you disrespected and you do not respond, she may feel unsafe with you. She finds some other guy and you make no babies. It's as simple as that.

Internally, self-importance is a defense against seeing the truth about ourselves. If we saw all of our shortcomings, we might want to jump off a bridge (and some of us do). So we lie to ourselves, using patterns of self-deception, blame, justification, deflection, and denial.

Self-importance is like a heavy suit of armor that wards off enemies. The problem is if we fall off our horse, we can't get back up again. And if we fall into the river, we drown. It's our evolutionary inheritance, but the question bears asking, "Is it a healthy adaptation?"

In *The Fire from Within*, the sorcerer Don Juan Matus tells apprentice Carlos Castaneda, "Self-importance is our greatest enemy. Think about it - what weakens us is feeling offended by the deeds and misdeeds of our fellow men. Our self-importance requires that we spend most of our lives offended by someone."

If we lessen our self-importance, we lessen our negative patterns and arrive at a place of self-worth, self-confidence, serenity, and contentment. Picture a wise, old Indian saint, seated on a raised platform. The world can hurl insults at him all day long. He doesn't care. He's not protecting a thing. He's just sitting there, and if you want to dump your anger all over him, it's okay with him. He has no self-importance, and yet everyone reveres him.

Let me paint a picture of self-importance for you. Neil is a 58-year-old suit-and-tie businessman, having a power lunch with other big shots at a fancy Manhattan restaurant. Neil accidentally spills some soup on the tablecloth in front of him. It's embarrassing. He hopes no one will notice.

Then along comes a busboy, who says to Neil, in a loud, sarcastic tone, "Hey, you made a mess on the table!"

What do you think Neil's response will be? Anger. More than anger - rage. He will probably start yelling and threatening lawsuits. He might even throw a punch or two at the guy, that is, until he keels over from a heart attack.

In the name of what? His self-importance.

Here's what was in his mind when he became enraged with the busboy:

- Shame: "Damn, he saw me spill the soup! Busted!"
- Fear of exposure: "Now everyone will see me for what I really am - a clumsy 9-year-old."
- More fear: "I'll probably lose the contract, and I've worked all year for it."
- Humiliation: "How dare he, a *busboy*, insult me, a big-time businessman!"

If we could observe our self-importance rather than react to slights to it, we'd all be happier, and the world would be a less violent place.

If you drill down to the heart of the matter, you'll see that out of the multitudes of negative patterns and emotions, they all boil down to *fear* and *shame*. Fear comes from the threat to our physical survival or integrity: "I'm not safe." Shame comes from the threat to our emotional/social integrity, which could get us thrown out of the group and cause us our life and our ability to procreate: "I'm not good enough. I'm bad." Once again, it's all about survival and procreation. Welcome to the human race!

Now that we understand a little about how we are hard-wired as animals, it will be much easier to see how, when, and why our own particular patterns developed in childhood.

The Formation of Our Patterns - Childhood Experiences

Negative patterns are usually set in place during our formative years. Our beliefs about the world, which help to form our patterns, become second nature to us between birth and elementary school age. This doesn't mean that we don't add, subtract, and revise beliefs and patterns throughout our lives. However, a lot of our current core beliefs and patterns track back to our childhood.

For example, 18-year-old Susan hides in her room a lot. Sometimes she even sleeps on the floor, wrapped in a couple of blankets. The behavior seems weird until you learn that Susan was molested by her grandfather when she was seven years old. The little kid that still exists in her needs the layers of blankets to feel safe and secure.

Then there's 37-year-old Giovanni, who can't ask women out on a date. His poor self-esteem and shyness are intimately connected to experiences of rejection he suffered as a child. In the 4th grade, Giovanni had been teased by the boys and girls for being chubby and odd. Those memories are still with him, the foundation of his inability to have a healthy social life.

As children, we all want to be loved, nurtured, cared for. It's rooted in our evolutionary need to be accepted by the group, in our need for self-importance. But at some point, usually in very early childhood, something thwarts us from getting our wants or needs met; something gets in the way. Perhaps someone criticizes or abuses us, or we feel misunderstood. The connection we want - usually with a parent, but it could also be with a grandparent, a sibling, an uncle or aunt, or another caretaker - is broken, at least for that moment. We react, doing what we can to try to get the love, nurturing, or attention we so desire.

What does that look like? Well, let's say as a 4-year-old you felt criticized and abused. You may have responded by acting the clown to get attention, or perhaps you learned to be seductive, or maybe you became a pleaser - trying to establish a connection with people by always giving them what they want, even at your own expense. You can visualize any of these methods as throwing hooks into a mountain to try to climb it.

When you still didn't get what you wanted, you then reacted in certain ways too. If you felt shut out, for example, you may have run away and hid or just felt bad for yourself. Or you may have become aggressive, reacting with anger that was really only masking the hurt you felt, and you threw darts the other way - blaming, attacking the other person, becoming aggressive or sarcastic or even passive-aggressive.

Here's an example. I worked with Michael, a successful businessman and lifelong drug addict, who loved marijuana, cocaine, opiates, and alcohol. Michael told me he was introduced to pot at age 13 by his best friend and liked the high.

But let's examine this a bit more. What did he mean that he liked the high?

"It relaxed me. Pot was the first thing I ever tried that made me feel...I don't know...mellow."

"Why did you want to feel mellow?"

"Everyone wants to feel mellow."

"But why you? Why was it important for *you* to feel mellow?"

At this point, Michael grew a little uncomfortable and literally squirmed around in his seat.

"Well, my house was a little crazy."

"It was?"

"My mom was kind of nuts."

"What did she do?"

"Lots of weird stuff. She used to walk around the neighborhood in her pajama bottoms, never put on make-up, and sang to herself."

"What about your dad?"

"He ignored her. Ignored everything. He died of a heart attack when he was 42."

Michael had a strange mother who probably had an undiagnosed mental disorder, and a disconnected father who checked out early from the family scene. Michael experienced a lot of anxiety and instability owing to an unpredictable, embarrassing, and occasionally volatile home life. One of Michael's negative patterns was control, a quite common response to drug-using, alcoholic, or otherwise unstable parents. The kid becomes parentified (made into a parent) and is forced to take over caring for the family.

Imagine that you're 11 years old, and running the show. What would you feel? Probably anxiety that you'd make a mistake and destroy the family, worry about your parents, constant tension, anger at your parents for being losers, fear that others would see what was going on in the home, and shame if and when they did.

As children, we develop at least a few, and possibly many, negative patterns. These patterns are often intertwined or overlapping. The man who is scared of his own shadow (*anxiety*) may try to command his little universe (*control*). He will display OCD symptoms, such as straightening out every little item in his little house. At the same time, he feels down (*depression*) about being stuck in the house (*isolation*) and not dating (*shame*). He doesn't date because he feels bad about himself (*low self-esteem*) and self-conscious (*embarrassment*) at his condition.

As you explore your own personality, you may find more than one negative pattern causing you problems. Don't be alarmed. Patterns, like wolves, travel in packs.

Think for a moment about how the events of your childhood affected you. How about the time your mom failed to pick you up from nursery school? You cried and cried, as if your world had fallen apart. At age four, it had.

Let's elaborate for a moment. Your mom tended to rush around, forgetful, anxious, hurried, worried about pleasing Dad, worried about pleasing everybody. She was an important role model for you, and you absorbed her thinking, feelings, and behavior. Remember, she was this way when you were in her womb, and perhaps you were chemically affected by her elevated stress hormones, by her surges of frustration and wrath, and her occasional tranquilizer and cigarette.

Mom modeled a whole bunch of beliefs to you:

- rushing around is good
- you should worry a lot
- be scared of others
- please others
- lose your temper now and then, and lash out at someone smaller than you

You learned:

- not to trust adults at all
- females act crazy a lot of the time
- you weren't as important as Dad
- you weren't as important as your mom's appointments
- you weren't worth very much at all

These were just some of the beliefs that you formed - and these were only in relationship to Mom. What about your interactions with Dad? With your older brother and sister? With teachers, schoolmates, and other family friends and relatives? Learnings from movies and television? From music? Each of these thought processes and beliefs were linked to emotions. Mom modeled worry, anxiety, fear, and anger. Your reactions to her included mistrust and self-hatred.

Now let's look at Dad and see how your beliefs about him shaped your worldview. Dad was a good guy. He played ball with you and took the family on great vacations. You still think fondly of trips to Disneyworld and Yellowstone, to see Cousin Dale and his wife, Myra, in Boston. Dad also got drunk at Cousin Rob's wedding, fell down in the living room, and broke the coffee table. Mom tried to help him up, but in his humiliation he grew angry and socked her in the eye with his fist. Mom went sprawling, dress over her head. You were shocked at their behavior.

Your dad modeled:
- drunkenness
- rage
- domestic violence
- shame

You felt:
- horror
- disgust
- embarrassment

What beliefs might you have developed from this single episode? (And chances are it happened on several occasions - it wouldn't be the only time you saw this particular scene played out in your childhood.)

You probably learned:

- it's okay to attack women
- it's okay to drink and lose control
- shame about Dad
- fear of Dad, perhaps generalizing to adult males or authority figures

These and other early experiences with Mom, Dad, and all of your other childhood influences led you to begin developing strong beliefs and emotions at a young age, based on your interpretation of life events. And here's the kicker: your early beliefs and emotions were *good*. In fact, they were brilliant!

If you developed a mistrust of authority figures because of your mom's unpredictability and your dad's violence, you were right to do so. No one should point a finger at you, and say, "Idiot, what were you thinking?" No one, including *you*. You were thinking like a normal, healthy 4-year-old: "Mom is whacky, and not to be trusted. Dad is dangerous when he drinks." Your thinking was logical and sound, and based on a built-in mechanism that served to ensure your safety and survival.

Why Patterns Persist

So it's a great thing, right? This tremendous ability that we, as human beings, have to form patterns for our own self-preservation - preservation of the physical as well as social/emotional self? So why do we need a book like this, teaching us how to get rid of these honorable things called patterns?

The reason is that what once served us as children has now become toxic. Patterns that protected us in childhood imprison us today - preventing us from having the things that would make us truly happy. If we're constantly protecting and defending or going on the offensive to feel important, we can't be open or connect with other people or take the risks necessary for growth and the pursuit of happiness.

Perhaps we can draw an analogy here. Our brain is still that of the hunter-gatherer, even though as a species we've moved into another phase of life. We don't have the same kinds of needs we did back then, yet our brain is still wired the way it always was. In the same way, the patterns that formed in us in childhood stay with us into adulthood though our needs have changed. It's important that we continue to evolve as a species, and as individuals.

Beliefs: How They Limit Perception and Shape Expectations

As we've seen, as a child you formed specific beliefs - thoughts you accepted as true. You repeated them over and over to yourself, hammering them into your conscious and unconscious minds. You still have a lot of those beliefs, though you've discarded some and picked up a few new ones along the way. You've created a *belief system*.

It is those beliefs that sustain your negative patterns. For example, if you believe, "God is watching every little thing I do," you might act in an upright, moral manner, but you may also experience a lot of guilt because you feel God knows all of your not-so-wonderful little moves.

Beliefs can get you into trouble. The debutante who believes, "Everything should always go my way," will find herself lonely and disliked by others who resent that their feelings are never taken into account. She will be disappointed when she begins to experience the truth that life cannot be controlled and things will not always go her way. Or how about the criminal who holds the belief, "Everyone better be nice to me all the time - or else!" He will get into bar fights, shootouts, knifings, beat-downs, jails, prisons, and hospitals. His belief has shaped his life. It has ruled it. And Lord knows how many more similar beliefs he has.

I knew a woman named Alice who was often depressed and gloomy. Granted, she had a history of trauma at an early age, and life was not easy for her. However, she constantly reinforced the belief that "Life is tough."

If you could have x-rayed her mind and seen her thoughts, they would have been:

- "I stink."
- "Everyone treats me like dirt."
- "Nothing ever works out for me."

These are the beliefs of a depressed person. Nothing ever works out for them - and nothing ever will. If it's true that what you believe is what you become, then a person who believes he is depressed will remain depressed and will create a life to be depressed about.

> "Man is made by his belief. As he believes, so he is."
>
> – Goethe

Our beliefs are based on perceptions. We experience something and make an interpretation of it. We decide if it is true or false, good or bad. In the simplest of terms, we look, we decide, and we believe. Suppose I look at Dad hitting Mom and I decide it is bad. I come to believe, "Men should not hit women." Of course, I might have looked at this and decided it was good, that men should not take any lip from women, that all men should be strong and bold, like Dad.

Perception is everything.

A turtle, walking down an alley, was jumped by two snails. Shook up, he went to the nearby police station, and excitedly told the detective what had happened.

The detective listened patiently to the turtle, and asked, "What did the snails look like?"

"I'm not sure," said the overwhelmed turtle.

"I need to know," said the detective. "Think."

The turtle, almost in tears, said, "I don't know. It all happened so fast!"

While we're on the topic of turtles and perception, when I was a kid, my cousin gave me a Mexican tortoise named Roy. I kept him in a large plastic tub (the tortoise, not my cousin) underneath our black-and-white TV set. I'd take Roy out now and then and let him roam around our tiny front yard, in reality a patch of ugly, yellowing grass and a single oversized shrub.

One day, I put Roy onto the grass and when I turned around, he was gone. Gone? Where could he have gone? The yard was maybe 15 feet deep by 10 feet wide, and Roy was amazingly slow, even for a tortoise. I think he needed a hip replacement. I looked near the bush, but didn't see him. I looked on the sidewalk. Nowhere to be found. An upsetting mystery. I never found Roy, though I looked and looked. Somehow, he had escaped down the street, down the block, managing to avoid cars, dogs, tough kids, and whatever other predators might have roamed the neighborhood.

Flash forward to a few years ago, and for some reason, Roy pops into my mind. The thought comes to me - *maybe he burrowed underground.* Can you believe it? It's 30 years later, and I'd never considered such an obvious possibility. You could argue that I was dumb and you could be right, but what was more interesting to me was that for all those years, I was only able to picture Roy walking above ground, and not going below.

My perception was limited. It was narrow, allowing me only one thought, one picture. I wonder how many other narrow perceptions I have that color my thoughts, emotions, and behaviors?

Our belief systems keep us stuck in limited perception, which keeps us stuck in our patterns.

A slight variation on this point about beliefs and perception is that they also shape our expectations. This is really important because, as visual creatures, we hold expectations in our mind in the form of images, and these images actually lead the way to creating what we get in life. You've heard of the Law of Attraction? The more we expect to get a particular result, the more we get that result, which reinforces our expectation to get it some more, and on and on. It's easy to see how beliefs and expectations become self-fulfilling prophecies. The way I relate to this is: "We are what we say we are."

My parents, for example, didn't have very high expectations for me or my siblings. They always assumed we would just go to Brooklyn College and settle down into some humdrum career. Yale and Harvard were never even considered. Nor was becoming the president of the United States. My parents' negative pattern here was poor self-esteem or a fear of success (we'll talk more about that later on). They didn't aspire to a higher station in life.

Well, I did end up going to Brooklyn College, as did my brother and sister, and my career started out very rocky. It took me a long time to find my way. My siblings and I have talked a lot about how we had to overcome the low expectations of our parents in order to create a more meaningful and fulfilling life. Popping our patterns and changing the images of ourselves that were planted in our brains by our parents was the primary work involved.

Patterns Provide Security

Another reason patterns linger is that they are familiar. As we've seen, one of the basic human needs is security, and patterns make us feel secure. You drive home from work the same way every day because it's a convenient route, but you also take comfort in the familiarity of the routine, the lack of surprise. The price you pay is boredom. The prize is a sense of safety.

Patterns soothe and comfort us,
but this is an illusion

Remember the set routines of Raymond Babbitt (the autistic brother played by Dustin Hoffman) in the movie *Rain Man*? Raymond *must* see his favorite TV show, which airs at a certain time each day. His brother Charlie

(played by Tom Cruise) ends up knocking on a farm-
house door in the middle of nowhere, pleading with a
housewife to let his brother watch the show. Raymond
will literally go nuts if he can't see "The People's
Court."

We all have routines and rituals. What are some of
yours? Do you have a sense of how and why they ini-
tially came about? I like to eat certain meals at a certain
time, drive certain routes home, and do certain activities on the weekend. There is, of course, the enjoyment
factor. I *like* those activities. But there's also something
comforting in predictable routines. It's the reason people
are often reluctant to change jobs, locales, and lifestyles.

The Transference Trap

A final reason patterns stay with us is that there is a
built-in mechanism for keeping us from getting to them.
This key perceptual dynamic, which causes many of
our problems, is transference. This is when we take our
(often unconscious) feelings and desires from childhood
and direct them toward people in our present lives, even
though they may not, in truth, apply. It really is a break
with reality. It's like we're looking at the world wearing
glasses whose lenses were given to us in childhood. We

are seeing the world, not as it really is, but through the "lenses" of our belief systems.

For example, I can work with a group in therapy and some clients will end up idealizing me, some hating me, when in truth I'm being the same with all of them. One client might see me as victimizing or bullying them, when that's really not what I'm doing. Another will see me as strong but loving. All the while, I'm just doing my best to hold up the mirror for them to see their patterns. I'm doing the exact same behavior, but each person is receiving my words and intentions differently based on their experiences, perceptions, attitudes, and so forth.

One such client got upset with me after a session, saying she didn't like me. I addressed the issue with her head-on. "It's fine that you don't like me, but I'm most interested in *why* you don't like me."

She said, "You remind me of a teacher I had. You cocked your eyebrow at me." She interpreted this body language as being dismissive, arrogant, and not caring.

Now it's true, I do raise my eyebrow sometimes. I asked her, "Would you like to know how it feels on my end?"

She said, "Sure."

I told her, "When I was younger I had a girlfriend who called me Spock because of the way I do that. A big part of me is left-brained, analytical, and I do that with my eyebrow when I'm really listening, analyzing, taking in information."

But just look at what she did with that.

Until we become aware of what we are doing while we're doing it, we are merely reacting to the world based on the lenses that were shaped by our belief systems, our life experiences, and our conditioning. Understanding this as fact forced me to be open to the possibility that, even though I think I am seeing something accurately, I may not be.

This conclusion has been reinforced for me time and again through one of the exercises I do with clients called "Poem/Dream/Story." The client writes a poem or dream, usually one that is recurring or compelling, and a story that can be autobiographical or fantasy. There are no specific rules. The content is important, but what's of equal value is *how* they approach the assignment, as this tells me a great deal about the lens through which they approach life - in other words, what their belief systems are.

For example, one person may think and think and then scribble down three lines, or someone may get up and leave the room, another person just goes and goes and writes outside of the lines, someone rhymes, someone else is free flowing, and so on and so forth. This will tell me so much about how they approach life and the beliefs that are contained there. It could be the perfectionist, "I'm going to do this wrong so I don't want to do this at all." It could show that anxiety is someone's underlying emotion. It can uncover that someone doesn't hear me at all, that they have selective hearing. This is a particularly interesting one. The client will do something totally different from the assignment I gave because they haven't heard my instructions. This helps me bring to their attention, "How are you hearing the rest of the world?"

I've had several clients tell me, "You're yelling at me," when I wasn't being sharp with them at all. I'll ask, "Was I really that way, or were you just hearing me that way?" Chances are these folks had an abusive or critical father, and since they are viewing me in a similar role (the transference), they were hearing me that way, even though I had *not* changed my tone. And yet the client doesn't see it at all.

Our early childhood patterns are still with us. This is such an important insight for people - they have lost the ability for introspection and, as such, have a distorted filter through which they look at and hear the world.

Where Patterns Show Up

Let's talk about where negative patterns show up. The easy answer is *everywhere*. Negative patterns impact all areas of our lives - work, social, romance, and family. But I'll tell you where they *really* show up: in couples and in families.

Imagine a guru on a mountaintop in the Himalayas. He's spent 40 years finding inner harmony and God. The guy is just *perfect*. That is, until he gets an email from his mother in New Jersey expecting him at family Thanksgiving. He starts to groan and grumble. Family! Thanksgiving! New Jersey! Oh, boy!

Or for those of you who are married, no one pushes your buttons like your husband or wife, right? It's the people we are closest to - who know us the best, who rile us the most, who can see past our stuff the easiest - that's who we struggle with.

But why is this so? Why are our patterns most apparent, at their rawest, with those people? I believe it's by spiritual design, that it's your spouse, parent, or sibling who helps you surface your negative patterns - surfacing them so they can be healed or transformed.

You can't diminish patterns until they've been surfaced, so you need something, or someone, to surface them. In other words, those button-pushers are really doing you a favor! Of course, it doesn't feel very good, but it's a favor nonetheless.

> People who surface your negative
> patterns are helping you

A great example of what I'm talking about is Carlos Castaneda's description of the "petty tyrant" in *The Fire Within:* "a tormentor . . . someone who either holds the power of life and death over warriors or simply annoys them to distraction." Don Juan tells Castaneda, "My benefactor used to say that the warrior who stumbles on a petty tyrant is a lucky one."

He further claims that the warrior's spirit is tempered by the challenge of dealing with petty tyrants - impossible people in positions of power. "To tune the spirit when someone is trampling on you is called control." Warriors use petty tyrants to get rid of their self-importance.

In much the same way, the button-pusher inadvertently helps us to recognize our patterns, and places us on the road to wholeness and well-being.

One of my faults is impatience. I am not the most tolerant guy on the planet. And that pattern is surfaced repeatedly in the supermarket. That's right - the supermarket.

One of my great triggers is the little old lady in the store line who *slowly* pulls the crumpled dollar bills out of her purse, drops a few coins on the floor, picks them up, realizes she isn't wearing her glasses, puts them on, *unhurriedly* flattens out the dollar bills - and while she's doing this, I'm hopping from foot to foot like a six year old who's got to pee his pants.

Instead of fuming and raging, I tell myself, "Hey, she's just an old lady. Have a little compassion. You're gonna be like her soon enough, pal!"

I reframe the scene and turn it into a comedy instead of a tragedy. "You've got to be kidding me! Are there hidden cameras around trying to catch me in a meltdown?"

From a spiritual vantage point, I remind myself that God is teaching me patience. This is all a lesson. In my mind I say, "Thank you," rather than awful, horrible things to the little old lady.

Everything serves to create patterns, which means *everything* helps us grow.

You will develop negative patterns, rest assured. The good news is that, with the right attitude, some mindfulness, and a little hard work, you can reduce or even remove them.

A Healthy Mindset for Popping Patterns: Seeing the Whole Truth

Part of seeing the truth about our patterns is being real with ourselves that we are not all that far off from the criminal who is behind bars, the drug addict seeking his next fix, the alcoholic mother about to slap her kid, or the white collar banker walking away with millions as his company implodes. We're too quick to minimize our patterns and too easy on ourselves.

Keeping an Eye on Your Patterns

Patterns should be treated like wild animals: know their power to harm you and give them the respect they deserve! What I've learned from my prison work is that if left unchecked, patterns have the destructive power to put any of us, as long as we are reactive and impulsive, behind bars or ruin our lives in some other way.

You don't agree?

As we learned in Chapter 1, we all have the same patterns, we just experience them and act them out to different degrees. And so you ask, "Well, how is it that I'm able to control myself, and criminals are not?" Let me answer this with a portrait of Francis, a half-white, half-Native American lifer, who is a composite of several inmates I've worked with.

As a boy, Francis had been raised by his grandmother after his junkie parents split for parts unknown. Grandmother was uncaring, and drank too much. At 11 years old, Francis was sent to juvenile hall, then to a boys' school. He was a good looking kid, and an older boy tried to rape him. The boy didn't get too far. Francis hit him in the mouth with a bottle, knocking out his teeth, and was sent back to juvenile hall.

Later Francis was drafted and sent to Vietnam. He became a machine gunner in a combat unit and was involved in numerous battles with enemy forces. Francis, like so many of his fellow soldiers, did things he was not proud of, terrible acts that scarred his soul. After Vietnam, Francis moved to Florida where he was approached by a low-level member of a New York crime family. They offered him big money just to mess up some guy he had never met before. Francis discovered that the work didn't faze him much. He had done much worse in Vietnam, and even in a few stateside bar fights.

Another contract was offered to him, and Francis accepted. This time it was to break a guy's right arm. Francis never learned why the right arm specifically, but he carried out the contract to the letter. Let's stop here before it gets too gruesome.

You're saying to yourself, "I would never do such a thing. I would never break someone's arm, let alone carry out contract murders." True. But you might defend yourself to the death if you were attacked. You certainly would defend your spouse or children if they were threatened. Killing to save yourself or your family doesn't seem far-fetched at all. You respond, "But that's protecting my family, and it's in the heat of the moment." Yes. But the point is that you have it in your psychic makeup to murder. You are capable of all sorts of actions. The real difference between you and the murderer is that you have been successfully conditioned *not* to murder. Why not?

> a) ***Fear of consequences***. If I murder, I'll end up in jail or prison.
>
> b) ***Fear of retribution***. If I murder someone, the victim's friends or family will come after me.
>
> c) ***Guilt and shame***. If I murder, my friends, family, and neighbors will shun me, judge me, be scared of me.
>
> d) ***Moral sense***. It's wrong to kill someone. My parents told me, my minister told me, everyone told me.

e) ***Positive reward***. If I behave properly, I'll receive praise, "You're a good boy."

Francis never had those same fears and conditioning. To the contrary, as a child he was filled with hatred for adults and authority, who were not to be trusted. Francis further learned that when he was passive, other people attacked him. No one defended him. He had to protect himself.

Francis learned at an early age:

- ✓ I have to be violent to survive.
- ✓ There's money and success in violence.
- ✓ People, including authorities (the U.S. government), *like me* when I'm violent.
- ✓ I'm good at violence.

Ask yourself this: "If I were brought up like Francis - no parents, societal indifference, abused by strangers, taught to kill - would I be able to murder?" The answer will likely be "Yes." Our prisons hold plenty of people who were otherwise "upstanding" citizens, but who, in the "heat of the moment" (in other words, in the "heat" of their pattern), committed a so-called "crime of passion." I'm sure you can think of a few examples!

Francis couldn't see his patterns - mistrust, anxiety, displaced anger, emotional disconnection, to name a few.

And because he couldn't see them, he couldn't change them.

Don't Be Too Hard on Yourself

The second part of seeing our patterns truthfully is not being overly *hard* on ourselves about them. People often want to berate themselves for their negative patterns. No! The goal is to *study* your faults. Identify them. Accept them, for the time being. But above all, don't judge them. Think about it: would you judge yourself if you had a broken toe? Gum disease? Hemorrhoids? I don't think so. You'd be in pain, and would seek help to fix the problem.

The problem with judging our patterns is that it very quickly becomes a warped, one-sided view. We forget all of our positives, and within about two seconds of focusing only on our negatives we feel like a completely worthless human being! Do you think this feeling will drive you to constructive action?

I ask clients to constantly look at judgments. I point out that judging is itself a pattern that holds us back. Judging actually distracts us from dealing with other patterns.

Truth-telling means having a balanced view of ourselves. Seeing the whole picture - the good and the bad, as it really exists. We will never be totally free of our patterns until we're dead or turn into Jesus, Buddha, or some other perfect human being. Once we work through one, five more show up on our plate. And that's okay, that's being human.

This book's method of popping patterns is firmly grounded in balancing our negative patterns with our positive ones, because with the perspective of our strengths in mind, the negative is a lot easier to work through. When we keep our successes in mind, we've got experience to draw upon in dealing with these negatives, which may otherwise feel overwhelming at times.

So, what I want you to do with your negative patterns after you've spotted them is *study them with neutrality*, and stay tuned for a way to remedy them.

Let me give you an example, to illustrate this crucial point:

Johnny is always late. He's a procrastinator. He turns up late for his brother's wedding and everyone's angry at him. He's disappointed and upset with himself. To forget his guilt, he drinks a lot. Because he drinks a lot, he feels guilty, and drinks even more. Then he wells up with anger at himself, along with guilt and self-pity.

Johnny is a mess, and the more he judges himself, the worse the problems get.

If a procrastinator judges himself, do you think he'll be more inclined to get out of bed and face the world, or more likely take a self-pitying turn for the worse, and say, "Ah, it's all gonna go wrong, I'll just stay in bed and deal with work and paying bills tomorrow"?

An alcoholic who judges himself will simply drink more, filled with self-disgust and guilt. The thing he feels guilty about - drinking too much - will be the thing he turns to diminish his guilt. Wow!

Don't beat yourself up for your shortcomings. Focus on taking action to change them. Neutrality is the antidote to harmful self-beating. View yourself with the dispassion of a scientist studying a cell. No blame, no "shoulds," no negative emotions. In the 12-step world, we take a fearless and searching moral inventory of our character defects. We do not take a fearful and angry look at ourselves.

Got it? Good. Now you're ready to take a look at some of the more common negative patterns.

CHAPTER THREE: Common Patterns

Now that we know what patterns are, let's look at some of the more common ones that frustrate and otherwise plague our lives. I could easily rattle dozens off the top of my head, but I'll start with five of the bigger ones - blame, self-pity, mistrust, low self-esteem, and complaining - which I see all too frequently in my clinical work.

Blame

Years ago, when my twin nephews were in diapers, my sister-in-law walked into the room and smelled something bad. For those of you who are parents, you know that smell - "stinky diaper."

Anyway, my sister-in-law walked over to the boys, who were identical twins, and said to the first twin, "Did you make in your pants?" First Twin looked up at her and shook his head no. She asked again, her eyebrows raised. "*Did* you make in your pants?" He looked up a second time, and again shook his head no. She asked, for the third time, "*Did you make in your pants?*" First Twin shook his head no, pointed at his twin brother, and said, "*He* made in my pants."

The ultimate blame story, right?

All human beings blame. It's a negative pattern that starts at an early age. We don't want to be wrong - God forbid! - because to be wrong means to be yelled at by Mom, Dad, Grandpa, Grandma, or the schoolteacher. We might even be punished or ostracized. To avoid this, we deflect responsibility onto others. "*I* didn't break the lamp. The dog did it!" Blame gets us off the hook.

Sal doesn't make his sales quota, and blames the lousy economy. "It's not *my* fault. It's the Fed…the interest rates…the housing crisis." Jeff tells his girlfriend he had five drinks at the bar because he was keeping Jimmy company. "Man, I didn't want to go, but Jimmy - you know how Jimmy is - he *made* me go. He *insisted*." Blame allows us to be irresponsible and unaccountable, just like kids. After all, it's not *my* fault if the cat pushed the delete button and lost my homework.

There's a great scene in *The Godfather* in which Don Corleone addresses his powerful fellow dons in a bank boardroom. Wanting to bring his son Michael home from Sicily, safe from all enemies, the Don tells the assembled Mafioso:

> I'm a superstitious man. And if some unlucky accident should befall [my son Michael], if he should be shot in the head by a police officer, or if he should hang himself in his jail cell, or if he's struck by a bolt of lightning, then I'm going to blame some of the people in this room, and that, I do not forgive.

Talk about accountability! These guys are accountable for *everything* that happens to Don Corleone's son. He will not allow them to blame anyone or anything else for harm coming to Michael.

Certain segments of our society won't tolerate blame or justification. The military is like that. You get up on time, eat on time, and - trust me - they really don't want to hear your rationalizations. Prison is much the same way. Correctional officers and their superiors are not interested in hearing inmates' excuses. In fact, they may even laugh in an inmate's face.

If you tend to blame, I recommend reading Don Miguel Ruiz's bestselling book, *The Four Agreements*. Prime among Ruiz's teaching is "being impeccable with your word." I love it! Blamers are *not* impeccable with their word. Their word is garbage. The good news is that blame is not the toughest pattern to break. I've seen blamers turn into accountable and successful people in no time at all. All they have to do is give up the pattern of blaming.

In addition to avoiding punishment, blame allows us to avoid looking at ourselves. If your boss critiques your performance, you can preserve your fragile ego by deflecting outwards. "I couldn't meet with Larson because Ramirez in Accounting made me call the Chrysler people. I told him the timing was bad, but you know how Ramirez gets." You'll do anything to avoid looking at yourself and admitting to possible character flaws. In this case, you have sidetracked your boss - but more importantly, you've sidetracked you.

Many negative patterns have developed around the desire to avoid looking at ourselves, somewhat under-standably. It can be a very painful process. As Jack

Nicholson shouted at the end of the film *A Few Good Men*, "You can't handle the truth!"

Sadly, we often can't...or choose not to.

Self-Pity

I remember once as a kid feeling bad for myself because my mom yelled at me. I ran into my bedroom and closed the door behind me, burying my head in my arms and bawling my eyes out. My secret hope - as with most self-pityers - was that my mom would come and apologize to me, that she'd be loving and gentle and confess the error of her ways.

Self-pity is, in a sense, a cry for love and understanding. Often this cry is ignored by others, which only creates more self-pity: "They aren't seeing my self-pity! Now I'm *really* feeling sorry for myself!" Self-pity goes hand in hand with victimhood, where the person plays at being a martyr. To that person, life is constantly "unfair."

Let's take Shelly, for example. She's standing outside a fashionable Manhattan restaurant, sweetly telling her friends, "I don't have enough money, but you guys go in without me. Have a good time." Shelly is a victim, filled with self-pity. The unexpressed thought here is, "I don't have enough. Poor me!"

A few other negative patterns are at play here as well:

Envy. Shelly thinks to herself, "Everyone has more than me. It isn't fair! I'm smarter than most of them."

Anger. In her mind, she screams, "You jerks! Thinking of yourselves, not of me. Just do what you want, and to hell with old Shelly!"

Entitlement. Shelly focuses on what she is lacking and the unfairness of it, rather than the fact that her friends want to go to this place. She should be pleased that they are able to afford this nice restaurant. But, of course, she isn't. She feels she should be entitled to go, too. She is entitled to everything.

Guilt. Shelly's words are intended to produce guilt. "Go in without me, have a good time," wishing, of course, that they will feel terribly guilty for leaving her out in the cold.

You know Shelly, don't you? Would you, by any chance, happen to *be* Shelly?

Anyway, here's what happens next. Her friends say, "Hey, no sweat, Shelly, come on in with us, we'll treat." But Shelly's pattern is victimhood. She loves it. It's what she does. It's what she knows best. She responds dramatically, "No, no, thanks, I don't mind waiting out here. I'll just grab a bite at the hotdog stand." On another day she might have angrily responded, "I don't need your charity. To hell with you!"

You can't win with Shelly. And her friends will undoubtedly figure it out sooner or later and vamoose. It's no fun hanging around with a martyr. To get out of the trap, Shelly could be assertive and loving. "Hey, guys, I can't afford this place, can we go somewhere else?" They'd probably say yes. But then without all the attention and fuss, it wouldn't be quite so much fun. Self-pityers have a weird sense of fun, you know.

Mistrust

It's not always a bad thing to be cautious and to have suspicions. Sometimes those suspicions are well-founded, as in the story of Jake, a Brooklyn guy, who comes home from work and is met at the door by his irate wife.

"What is this piece of paper in your pocket I found," she demands, "with the name 'Esmeralda' on it?"

"What are you hockin' me for?" he protests. "Esmeralda is the name of a horse I bet on."

She grumbles, doesn't quite believe him.

Jake goes out bowling for the evening with his buddies, stays out until midnight. As he walks through the front door, his wife smacks him in the head.

"Hey," he cries, "what was that for?"

"Your horse called!"

People who are inordinately and constantly suspicious of others have an issue with trust. This pattern is often a distorted by-product of early experiences with early caregivers who disappointed or betrayed them. Continued mistrust, however, results in separation from others, and that is unfortunate.

It is important to be cautious and to exercise good judgment in dealing with others, but there is a time to have faith, to take a leap, to believe in someone. The mistrustful person is scared to take that leap, and cowers in the corner, alone, afraid, and bitter.

Low Self-Esteem

Low self-esteem begins in childhood. We think poorly of ourselves as the result of critical messages from parents, siblings, friends, the world at large, or what we have *interpreted* as critical messages. Whether the criticism was real or we just took it that way, we still get the same result - a low opinion of ourselves and feelings of unworthiness.

This pattern is particularly difficult because it becomes self-sustaining. Long after anyone else is putting us down, we continue do it to ourselves through our own terrible self-judgments. Feeling bad about ourselves actually feels *normal*. And because it's what we're used to, we keep it going - all by ourselves. Ain't that a kick?

Dr. Howard Liebgold writes in *Freedom from Fear*, "We incorporate all that negativity into our self-talk. We no longer need enemies or adversaries. We become our own worst enemy, repeatedly voicing a myriad of negative labels."

Low self-esteem is often the underlying issue for the criminal or the drug addict. The only way out is a new self-image - the sinner must become a saint, the villain a hero.

Do you know how I became a doctor? By intending it. I had to change my self-definition from "loser, nobody, jerk" to "doctor, healer, success." I did this by telling myself that I *was* a healer. I self-talked my way to success.

Complaining

The complaining person is a victim who whines, blames, and is always in a dependent, or childlike position, pointing a finger at authority figures.

After all, it's much easier to complaint than to actually do something. The complainant/victim is also very self-righteous. "Did you see what they did to me?" It's a position of profound weakness and the antidote (as with several other allied patterns) lies in assumption of responsibility. Run your life, take action, make choices, without complaint, and a willingness to abide by the consequences of those choices.

To illustrate the pattern, there was once a young mother at the beach, playing with her toddler at the water's edge, when all of a sudden, out of nowhere, a giant wave came and snatched the child away.

The frantic mother got down on her hands and knees, and begged, "God, Master of the Universe, you who have the power of life and death, please, I beseech you, bring my child back!"

As if on command, the giant wave returned and gently deposited the unharmed and giggling toddler onto the sand at his mother's feet.

The mother looked up at the sky and snapped, "He had a hat."

Patterns...by Category

Let's look through the following list of negative patterns of thought, emotion and behavior and get a sense of which are most prominent for you. This list is by no means exhaustive. It may be, in fact, that we discover and name a few new patterns during the course of our work together!

While patterns may appear to be similar, they are not necessarily identical to one another. Like colors in a wheel, there are subtle differences in shades and hues.

For instance, Dictionary.com defines aggression as "any offensive action, attack, or procedure." Intimidation, however, has a slightly different meaning: "to force into or deter from some action by inducing fear." The former is active and the latter is passive.

By way of example, Jerry is aggressive. He is loud, his body language is angry, and he gets red in the face at a business meeting. Bob, on the other hand, is intimidating: at the business meeting he calmly comments that if they don't follow his lead, he'll sue the pants off of them.

Negative patterns fall loosely into five discrete categories. These are distinct and habitual modes of responding
to stress and/or satisfying our desires. At their core, these
are survival strategies, enabling us to cope with life.

- Domination
    - Attack
    - Entitlement
    - Control
- Defense
    - Block
    - Counterattack
- Submission
    - Anxiety
    - Depression
    - Dependence
    - Guilt & Shame
- Flight
    - Disconnect
    - Avoidance
- Freeze
    - Invisibility
    - Immobility

In nature, animals react in instinctive ways to stressors such as hunger, thirst, and the threat of predators.

They attempt to satisfy their needs, such as the acquisition of a mate through attack, defense, submission, flight, or freezing, depending on their genetic makeup and the specifics of the situation.

Here are some examples of the five categories as they appear in nature:

- ✓ A lion <u>dominates</u> through aggressive gestures and a powerful roar.
- ✓ A rat <u>defends,</u> if cornered.
- ✓ A dog <u>submits</u> to a larger or more aggressive dog by rolling on its back and showing its belly.
- ✓ A mouse <u>flees</u> from a cat.
- ✓ A deer in the woods <u>freezes</u> and is camouflaged from predators by trees, branches and leaves.

What is your default position with regard to threat? Does it vary from situation to situation, or does it tend to be the same?

As you examine your patterns, themes may emerge that highlight your typical responses to needs and stressors. Be aware that there are no right, wrong, good, or bad responses, but only efficient ways to respond to their dictates.

Domination

The message common to all forms of domination is "I want what I want" and am prepared to get it by overt or covert means, and the threat or commission of violence. Domination is an expression of *power*. The predominant emotion associated with this position is anger (fury, rage, frustration, annoyance, ire, etc.).

Attack

This is an active position, fueled by your desire to get your needs met. You wish to frighten others into submission. There is the threat of violence, or actual violence, either physical or verbal.

The attack position may be innate (the attacker is born with a predisposition towards threat or violence) or learned (he identifies with an abuser and becomes an abuser himself, submerging feelings of pain and hurt and displaying anger toward others).

Aggressive. Glare at others, violent-hostile undercurrent.
Bullying. You push others around in a show of size and force.
Intimidating. Make others feel frightened or insecure.
Oppositional. A rebel without a clue.

<u>Paranoid</u>. Everyone is out to get you.

<u>Profane.</u> Use bad language to assert yourself, show how tough or bad you are.

<u>Sarcastic.</u> Attack verbally with pointed, cutting comments.

Entitlement

You please yourself first, a selfish and immature stance. You want to know, "What about *me*?" It is not as active nor as violent as Attack, but there is a constant threat of explosion. Attack mirrors the actions of a fierce animal; Entitlement is more like the actions of a squalling infant who insists on being fed or held.

<u>Arrogant.</u> You're a know-it-all and cannot be told what to do.

<u>Attention-seeking</u>. Must be visible, needs to be noticed.

<u>Demanding</u>. You insist on getting what you want.

<u>Entitled</u>. The world owes you.

<u>Grandiose.</u> Inflated sense of self - you are the king.

<u>Histrionic.</u> Dramatic, wants to be center of attention.

<u>Lazy.</u> Others take care of you.

<u>Narcissistic.</u> Consumed with your own self, lacking empathy for others.

<u>Self-absorbed.</u> Selfish, focused on your own needs and wants.

Control

This subcategory is a bit less visible than Attack or Entitlement, but the goal is the same: to dominate others and get what you want. Violence is used less, but implied more. Machiavelli, the famed 16th century court advisor, was an archetypal Controller, teaching princes how to vanquish and subjugate people and nations.

Controlling. Pull others' strings, have it your way.

Deceptive. Present a positive image to mask malicious thought or behavior.

Manipulative. Split people, cause others to take sides, gossipy.

Negotiator. Want to make a deal with others and get the better of them.

Seductive. Try to manipulate others with sex or sensuality.

Defense

This position is a response to domination in the form of either a Block (an attempt to stop the attack) or a Counterattack. The latter may appear in nature as a last resort for non-predators who feel trapped or cornered. The emotions most associated with this position are anxiety coupled with anger: "You have scared me and I will fight back!" Other messages include, "You won't take it from me," and "If you take it from me, I will punish you as a deterrent so that you won't be so quick to harass me in the future."

Block

Defend. Can't bear the truth, push it away.

Justify. Always explain why you had to do what you did.

Mistrustful. Extremely cautious, skeptical, do not believe others.

Rationalize. You find good reasons for the crummy things you do.

Counterattack

Blame. It's never your fault, it's always the other person's fault.

Passive-aggressive. Your smile hides your crummy behavior.

Rebellious. Lash out against authority.

Resentful. Sullen, quiet, angry, feel put upon.

Vengeful. You've been injured and want to hurt your opponent.

Submission

Submission is a passive position. You are fearful, worthless, reliant on others, or have simply given up.

Submission is an expression of *powerlessness*. Perhaps you hope that the predators will leave you alone if you roll over on your back. Often this works. However, a reliance on the good will of others may sometimes result in being used or hurt by them.

Anxiety

You feel threatened by the world around you - people, places, and things. You have a constant fear of others and the harm that they will do to you.

Anxious. Nervous, agitated, worried.

Hyperemotional. Excessively reactive, bordering on the hysterical.

Interrupting. Scared of not being heard.

Orderly. Everything must be just-so, well laid out, well planned.

Perfectionist. Must do it right at all times, cannot make mistakes.

Procrastination. Fear of failure, success or change.

Stuck. Unwilling to take chances, paralyzed.

Verbose. Talk too much, or too often, in order to relieve anxiety.

Depression

You feel helpless and hopeless, the victim of circumstances, a deckhand on the ship of life rather than the captain. You just know that it's not going to work out, and guess what? It never does.

Defeatism. You give up before you start.

Depressed. Low energy, sad, feeling down.

Helpless-hopeless. Nothing is ever going to work out for you.

Powerless. Weak, whiny, timid.

Self-destructive. You harm yourself in physical or material ways.

Self-pity. You feel bad for yourself and cry for yourself because no one else will.

Self-sabotaging. You harm yourself mentally and emotionally, seeking failure instead of success.

Victim. Whine, complain, blame others, rail against fate.

Dependence

You want to feel protected, and you will try different ways of getting that need met.

Approval-seeking. Want to be reassured that you are okay.

Caretaking. Help others compulsively.

Clinging. Needy, annoying, won't let go.

Dependent. You rely on the kindness of others.

Ingratiating. Want to be accepted and valued by giving too much.

Over-polite. Exceedingly pleasant, rarely angry.

Passive. Go along with everything, do not speak up for yourself.

People-pleasing. Take care of others, to gain their liking.

Guilt and Shame

You've been criticized, demeaned, or abused your entire life. Like the anxious person, you fear attack at any moment; like the depressed person, you view the world in a negative light. You may present a "normal" false front while inwardly feeling worthless or assume a submissive posture, e.g., hang your head, avert your eyes, etc.

Guilty. You have done something bad.

Low self-esteem. Think poorly of yourself.

Shameful. You are something bad.

Flight

The message of the person in flight is "You won't catch me." You run from internal and external dangers. The former often takes the form of frightening emotions or impulses such as anger, rage, lust, or violence; the latter may consist of threats from a Dominator.

Disconnect

Somewhere down the line, you learned that feelings were bad, or felt overwhelmed by feelings. You've learned to compartmentalize or ignore your emotions, and react with numbness or conversely, hyperactivity to block these feelings.

Denial. You fail to see the truth of what is going on around you.

Emotionless. Numb, no feeling, stoic, very little facial movement.

Intellectualize. Block off emotions by being cerebral.

Joking. Overly playful, silly behavior.

Manic. Excessive energy, hyperactivity.

Minimize. Nothing is a big deal. You make little of large events.

<u>Suppression.</u> Submerge your true thoughts and feelings.

<u>Thrill-seeking.</u> Engage in risky behaviors, such as criminal activities, drug use and unprotected sex.

Avoidance

<u>Desertion</u>. You pack your bags and go.

<u>Hiding</u>. In plain sight or out of view.

<u>Isolation</u>. You don't come out of your room.

<u>Quitting</u>. You fail to stick with things.

Freeze

This mode, too, is associated with anxiety. However, the anxiety here may be so pronounced that it is more accurately typified as "terror." Do you know the feeling of being stuck in a dream, chased by a horrible monster, unable to wake up?

You want to be invisible. The message is, "Please don't see me." Your movements and facial expressions may reflect this: an absence of gesture, mannerism and affect, or a permanent grin.

In nature, your animal is the possum, who will play dead in order to fool predators. You learned a long time ago that if you are immobile, they will (perhaps) leave you alone.

The important difference between Flight and Freeze is that the former is active, the latter passive. The fleeing person tries to get away from the Dominator while the frozen person hopes to avoid being seen by remaining immobile.

Invisibility
<u>Invisibility</u>. You lack color so as not to be noticed.
<u>Looking good.</u> Must always appear polished and attractive, but your features are rigid, a constant smile.

Immobility
<u>Motionless</u>. You do little and desire less.
<u>Soundless</u>. You are a quiet and ghostlike presence.

Now that you've read through the categories and patterns, make a list of all the ones that grabbed your attention. Then, number those from one to ten, one meaning that you really identify with that pattern, and ten meaning that you only have a little bit of identification with that specific pattern.

You're starting to get a sense of what you need or want to work on.

Fear and Anger

While fear and anger are emotions and not patterns, they are linked frequently to many of the negative patterns listed above. Let's take a look at the role of fear and anger in the production and maintenance of negative patterns.

Three Fears

We all have fear – of people, places, things, situations, ourselves, and so forth. There is nothing wrong with fear, and in fact, it often serves a useful purpose, as illustrated in the following story.

The famous British admiral, Lord Nelson, was in his flagship at sea, sleeping soundly in his cabin when he heard the first mate banging loudly on the door.

"Admiral," yelled the mate, "please, come at once!"

Nelson rushed to the deck. The mate handed him a large telescope. Looking out onto the horizon, Nelson spotted an enemy warship.

In the calmest voice possible, Nelson instructed the mate, "Bring me my red shirt."

The puzzled mate did as requested. Nelson casually put on the shirt, and moments later, the enemy ship sailed away.

"Admiral," said the mate, "please, sir, why did you want me to bring you the red shirt?"

"Simple, Benson. If we were attacked, and I was wounded, I would not want the men to see my blood and be demoralized."

"Right, sir!" beamed the mate, proud of his brilliant Admiral.

The following morning came a loud banging on the Admiral's cabin door. It was the first mate, shouting.

"Admiral, come at once, sir!"

As Lord Nelson rushed up the stairs, the first mate handed him a telescope. Nelson looked out at the horizon, and saw a hundred enemy warships.

"Benson," he said with exaggerated calm.

"Yes, sir?"

"Bring me my brown pants."

There are many types of fears connected to patterns: fear of being visible and conversely of being invisible and unheard; fear of being hurt, fear of being rejected, fear of being betrayed, fear of not having enough or being deprived. All of these are worth exploring with the client.

The argument could be made that every pattern has a fear associated with it. For instance, bullying. The bully seems fearless, but in fact is scared of being seen as weak and pushed around by others and so he in turn pushes others around. Chances are he was pushed around by someone bigger and stronger, such as a parent, sibling, relative or neighbor.

People-pleasers are scared that others will abandon them and do everything they can to ensure that others will stick around by taking care of their needs.

Helpless and hopeless folk are frightened of doing something wrong and so they don't do anything at all, but have others do it for them. Or, perhaps they are scared of being successful.

Fear of success, in fact, is one of three specific fears I encounter on a regular basis in my work. The other two are fear of failure and also of change.

Barbara was a 24-year-old fitness instructor who had flunked out of college and was financially dependent on her well-to-do family. She had lots of bad habits, among them speeding around town in her brand-new sports car. Her mother nagged her constantly to get a "real career," and her dad mostly shook his head and scowled in disappointment.

Barbara liked zipping in and out of traffic ("It's fun"), not too worried about the speeding tickets, which she tucked away in her car's glove compartment. Out of sight, out of mind.

When I asked her about this, she said, "I meant to pay them."

"But you didn't."

"I guess I procrastinate a lot."

"Why?"

"I don't know."

"Could it be because you'd have to tell your parents about it? That'd they have to pay?"

"My dad would definitely have to pay. And he'd kill me!" *Bingo!*

In Barbara's case, what looks like procrastination is really a fear of failure, of criticism, of being rebuked and chastised by a critical father.

Barbara was like the 2 year old who steals the cookies and accidentally breaks the jar, then sweeps all the pieces under the rug, figuring that no one will notice the big, unsightly, bulge under the living room carpet.

It ain't much of a plan, but then, hey, it ain't bad for a 2 year old.

Fear of Failure

We are scared to fail. That's understandable. If we fail, we believe we are defective, lacking - in short, we experience shame. We think to ourselves, "If I fail, I'm a loser, I'm no good."

Some people are perfectionistic. They try and try, but never seem to turn in the project - and that way they never fail. I often encounter clients who have managed to avoid doing things just so that they don't have to deal with feelings of failure.

Carla, for instance, tells me that she wants a better paying job.

"I want to be a lawyer, Dr. K."

"And right now you're a paralegal?"

"Yeah. But I'd really like to be a lawyer."

So far, so good. She wants the prestige, money, and challenge that go along with being an attorney.

"So what's stopping you, Carla?"

"Nothing."

"Good. Did you apply to law school?"

A slight frown. "No. Not yet."

"But soon?"

Something is stopping her from applying to law school.

"Well. I don't know. I mean, I want to."

"But?"

"I have to take the LSAT."

"You can take the LSAT, can't you?"

"Yes and no."

More specifically, something is stopping her from taking the test for law school.

"What's the yes?"

"Well, I'm smart, and I do have a good grasp of the law."

"And the no?"

"What if I don't pass?"

"You'll take it again."

"Yeah." Hesitant. "What if I fail?"

She is frightened of failure.

"What's so horrible about failing?"

"I hate it."

"Haven't you ever failed at anything before?"

"Yeah. I can't stand it."

"Look. Lots of people fail bar exams, medical boards, psychology boards, and then they pass later. It happens all the time."

As we talk some more, I learn that Carla is a perfectionist. At an early age, she made up the rule, "I cannot fail. Failing would be intolerable." It's a belief that developed during her childhood. Carla's parents had demanded perfection in sports and academics. Her room had to be spotless. Failure was not acceptable.

Carla equates failure with shame - being bad and worthless.

Because failure is always a possibility in anything we try, if a person is unable to face the possibility of failing, they become paralyzed. They cannot take action. They cannot go forward. Carla could not take her test for law school because of the possibility of failure.

This negative pattern of *perfectionism* showed up glaringly in all areas of her life, including vocation. As I came to know Carla better, I learned that she rarely dated because few men met up to her standards. She had few friends, for the same reason.

Carla's negative pattern was ruining her life.

We worked on her perfectionism daily. I had her purposely fail at any number of tasks. I gave her the tasks of having a sloppy room, keeping a messy kitchen, and handing in a mediocre assignment at work. What she needed was not to pass the LSAT, but rather to be okay with less-than-perfect performance.

Have you ever watched a 5-year-old try to hit a baseball? Sometimes they can't do it. Rather than pressure them and grow frustrated with them - which will only make *them* feel pressured and frustrated - it's better to help them to relax. I encourage the kid to miss the ball. To purposely *not* make contact. To swing soft, to swing hard, to laugh, to be silly. To have a good time.

After awhile, I'll suggest that he tap the ball. Just make contact. Nothing more. I'll keep the whole thing light. No big kudos for tapping the ball, no pressure or harsh words for missing the ball. In fact, I may misdirect the kid. Rather than making it about tapping the ball at all, I'll tell him that what we're doing is "trying to get the ball back to me. See if you can get it back to me by throwing it. Or kicking it. Hey, I've got an idea. How about *hitting* it back to me?"

So many of our greatest thinkers, inventors, and leaders experienced failure after failure until they achieved success.

There is a well-documented story about a man who endured numerous failures. He was defeated in a run for the state legislature, failed in business, had a nervous breakdown, was defeated as state house speaker, defeated in a run for congress, got elected but lost the renomination, rejected for a land officer position, was defeated in a run for the U.S. Senate and then the vice presidency, and defeated again in a run for Senate. He eventually won an election though and in 1860 Abraham Lincoln became the 16th president of the United States.

I often tell people that I've stumbled my way to success. Whenever I tried too hard, I failed. Whenever I was fluid and open, success came easily. If we can shift our focus from perfection to continuous improvement, we will keep moving forward. Guaranteed!

Fear of Success

This is a hard one for a lot of people to accept. "Why would anyone be scared of success?" they demand to know. And yet I know plenty of folk who are terrified of succeeding. In fact, I probably run into more people who are scared of success than are scared of failure.

Think about it. If you succeed, you become a target of envy. Your friends, neighbors, relations, and colleagues want what you have. They may vilify you, saying nasty things about you behind your back or even to your face. This bothers us. You bet!

Fear of success makes sense from an evolutionary psychology standpoint. Because if the group doesn't like us - if they are envious or jealous - they may throw us out of the cave and we'll be forced to face hungry saber-toothed tigers.

Have you heard of the Tall Sunflower Syndrome? It's a well-known phenomenon in England, and basically states that the tallest sunflower - the one that towers over the others - will be chopped down. The fear is that if we're visible, we're going to get chopped down, ostracized, targeted, thrown out of the group.

Tell the truth: isn't it comfortable to conform, to go along with the others? Successful people are often alone, a frightening and uncomfortable position to assume. Many of us would rather stay down than be up there by ourselves. It takes a great deal of inner strength to be apart from the crowd.

There's another reason why some of us fear success, and that reason is shame. We may not feel that we deserve success. In our heart of hearts, we feel unworthy of receiving good things. The pattern of self-sabotage is frequently visible with my shame-based clients, who refuse to have success. As soon as you give them money, a good job, a great relationship, they mess it up.

There is a famous quote on this topic by author Marianne Williamson in her book *Return to Love*, as follows:

> Our deepest fear is not that we are inadequate. Our deepest fear is that we are powerful beyond measure. It is our light, not our darkness that most frightens us. We ask ourselves, "Who am I to be brilliant, gorgeous, talented, fabulous?" Actually, who are you not to be? You are a child of God. Your playing small does not serve the world.

There's nothing enlightened about shrinking so that other people won't feel insecure around you. We are all meant to shine, as children do. We were born to make manifest the glory of God that is within us. It's not just in some of us; it's in everyone. And as we let our own light shine, we unconsciously give other people permission to do the same. As we're liberated from our own fear, our presence automatically liberates others.

We don't want to be seen in our glory because we don't want to be visible. We don't want to be visible because we've been taught by our society and our parents, "Be modest and humble. Don't get too big for your britches."

Fear of Change

I worked with a group home girl named Ashley, whose father had broken her arm in a fit of anger. It turned out that he had been abusive to her on several occasions, and the Department of Children and Family Services had placed her in foster or group homes at various times.

In planning out her next steps, Ashley told me she wanted to go back with her dad. She had no mother and did not want to live with her grandmother. I suggested she go into a long-term program. She refused.

"But your dad hurt you."

"He didn't do it on purpose."

"You told me he was angry, and he was drinking."

"I should have stayed out of his way instead of arguing with him."

We went around and around until she finally told me, "Dr. K., the thing is, I know my dad. I know what he does, what he might do. I don't know these other people."

Just like the old folk saying, "Better the devil you know than the devil you don't."

We all know people who have never moved out of their neighborhood and barely visited other cities or states, let alone other countries. If asked about this, they will say, "I have everything I need right here," or "It takes too much money, effort, hassle." The truth is that they are scared of the unknown.

> We are frightened of change

There is a great line in the 12-step world about the definition of insanity: "Doing the same thing over and over again and expecting a different result." Isn't this a perfect description of a pattern? We may repeat ourselves constantly, even when it's not working because the devil we know is better than the one we don't.

I said it before - patterns, routines, and habits are *comfortable*. They're easy. They make us feel safe. Change is difficult. It's *uncomfortable*. But so necessary, if we want to get those things in life that we truly desire. The choice is ours.

Understanding Anger

We ask, what is the relationship of anger to negative patterns of thought, emotion and behavior?

Anger is the prime emotion of the Domination category. The aggressive person either feels, or feigns, anger to get his needs met. The Defender grows angry, or aggressive, in response to a threat from a Dominator.

The Submissive, Flight or Freeze people tend to deny their anger. They bottle it up and stuff it, and then claim, "I don't have any anger."

Is that true? Not in my book. They simply don't like feeling angry or confronting others. They explain this away with the bogus claim of not feeling anger.

In truth, they made up their minds a long time ago that:

1. Anger is bad – I don't want to experience it

2. I've seen what anger does, and want no part of it
3. If I'm aggressive, I'll end up getting destroyed
4. It feels weird to feel angry
5. If I lose my temper, I'll probably kill someone

You can see how hard it would be to express anger if you held on to some or all of these beliefs.

The Dominator and Defender need to learn how to control, regulate and channel their anger. The Submissive, Flight and Freeze people need to learn how to allow themselves to have it, and then express it in an appropriate way.

But first they've got to understand anger, starting with why we have anger. Stated differently, what is below our anger?

In my therapy work, especially within the prison system, I have encountered many people who were very angry. They revealed to me time and again the four principal underlying causes of anger:

1) Fear (or anxiety, worry, nervousness)
2) Hurt (often of the betrayal kind)
3) Humiliation (from being disrespected), which ties into shame
4) Cognitive differences

This perhaps links back to evolutionary psychology. Fear in the ancient world *should* produce anger because it creates the energy needed to take action. If I'm scared of the saber-toothed tiger, my body will react accordingly and assist in my survival. The physiology of anger is the same physiology as the response to threat - "fight or flight."

As for hurt or betrayal, we're social animals. It's not okay to be betrayed in a group situation because in olden times that meant our survival was threatened. Humiliation is also problematic. If we're made to look bad, it could jeopardize our ability to find a mate and perpetuate our genes which, from an evolutionary standpoint, is our primary purpose in life.

Cognitive differences operate on the thought level. If we hold a belief that differs from another person, we may be angry or frustrated when they fail to comply with our wishes. We slip into "should" mode: "He should not litter," "He should watch out for me," "She should know that I have the right of way."

You've probably seen this when you talked politics, sports or religion with your neighbor. All of a sudden you felt yourself getting hot under the collar and thinking, "That guy is an idiot," just because he disagreed with you.

A challenge to our thinking is an affront or attack against our self-importance. If we are truly tolerant of others, we'll have few if any cognitive differences – no clashing beliefs or values with others.

The key to anger is to see where it's coming from, work it all the way through rather than minimize it, and decide if you want to diminish or eradicate it completely.

Let's look at the Attack subcategory. This person wants to fight with others, frighten them, or control them as a way to feel powerful and important. He may assault or intimidate others in order to ensure his own survival, like Graves, a 47-year-old inmate, doing time for an armed robbery. Graves wants respect. Getting and keeping respect in prison is very important. It can literally save your life. It may seem like Graves is just a bully, glaring at people, putting out a tough vibe, but he has to intimidate in order to survive the prison yard. "Anybody look at me sideways, I'll bust him in the head." He is talking about the threat of disrespect, or humiliation.

Ramona is a 38-year-old housewife from suburban Los Angeles. She is sarcastic - a verbal bully. "I can't stand listening to other people. They're so dumb! It drives me nuts. I get totally frustrated." She attacks because she was often criticized and verbally assailed as a kid. You might say she learned to defend by attacking, sort of like the old sports adage, "The best defense is a good offense." But let's look under the surface of her anger. The emotion at work is fear. Ramona feels under siege all of the time.

Let's say your wife teased you at a party in front of your friends. You felt betrayed by her. The "attack" was unexpected. Or you told your coworker that you were looking for another job. He promptly told the boss, who called you in and gave you a hard time. You were furious with your coworker. You felt hurt and betrayed. You trusted him, and he let you down.

Think of a time when you felt angry and then look below the surface. Consider why you were *really* angry.

> Below anger lies hurt,
> fear, or shame

Here's an example of an Attacker I knew very well: my father, Henry Kadish, who passed away only a few years ago.

Dad grew up Jewish in Nazi Germany (the family was originally from Russia). His father, Bernhard, was taken away by the Gestapo in 1935, never to be seen again. This tragedy was compounded by the subsequent death of an infant brother. His mother, Celia, was placed in a sanitarium on the heels of this terrible double loss. Family legend had it that she had a breakdown of sorts, perhaps mental, physical, or both.

Dad was placed in an orphanage for Jewish children in the small town of Dinslaken, outside of Dusseldorf. An angry, skinny 10-year-old, Dad became so enraged that he ripped a porcelain washroom sink out of the orphanage's bathroom floor. Grandma, Dad, and his sister, Paula, reunited and managed to escape Nazi Germany in July 1938, just before the gates closed, and came to America.

Let's skip ahead to the late 1950s and early 1960s. We lived in a tiny row house in Canarsie, Brooklyn. Dad was a good father, very involved with my brother Brian, sister Amy, and me. He played games with us, read poetry and sang to us, had us listen to classical music. He would march us around the living room to military music. (He'd served in the Navy during WWII, which could explain some of this.) It was fun for us kids, but also an indication of Dad's need for control and order.

Dad would rage at Mom and the kids if things weren't just so. He could be critical, and expected a great deal from his children. If he disagreed with our point of view, he ran us over. Dad could be very self-righteous. "Don't be stupid! Republicans are all greedy bastards!"

What I'm painting here is a picture of a wounded, angry boy, who barely escaped with his life from a dangerous, hostile environment. He became the man of the family at the age of 12, and thereafter made the majority of financial and life decisions for the family.

Surely Dad felt powerless as a child - frustrated, anxious, and full of rage. Those beliefs and emotions translated into patterns of control and displaced anger, which were played out with his wife, children, and friends. His patterns were the product of the experiences he'd had as a child, or more precisely, his interpretation of those experiences.

Here's a tip: when you see someone acting intimidating, bossy, or aggressive, get out of their way if you can. But also take a moment and reflect on the forces that shaped them.

It's important to reflect on our patterns, and the patterns of others. It's only through understanding ourselves and others that we can achieve a measure of peace in our lives.

Furthermore, if someone you are talking to becomes angry during your conversation, instead of reacting in a defensive manner, ask yourself: "What's really being expressed by this person's anger? What's *below* the anger? Do they feel disrespected, humiliated, or betrayed? Threatened or violated?" Becoming aware of what lies beneath anger can help us be more effective when resolving conflicts with someone while they're angry.

The Magnificent Seven

I'd like to end this chapter about patterns with a quick look at my favorite movie of all time, *The Magnificent Seven*. (Studying movies, by the way, is a fun and effective way of identifying negative patterns.) I've seen the film dozens of times, and am one of the few people you'll ever meet who can name all seven actors and tell you their character names, too! I highly recommend it for deepening your understanding of patterns, even if you're not inclined to watch old films.

Each of the seven main characters has a particular strength and a particular flaw. Chico (the kid) thinks he is a gunman, but is really a farmer. He is a *self-loather* who despises himself for being one of the peasants he's protecting. Bernardo also has *poor self-esteem*. He tells the village kids assigned to look after his needs that their fathers, unlike him, are truly courageous. He shrugs off his talents and abilities. Harry's *greed* eventually kills him. Vin *self-sabotages* with gambling and aimlessness. Britt is a Zen poet in a Wild West setting, sitting cross-legged and studying the petals of a flower while calmly awaiting a shootout. Britt shoots a bandit from a horse at 200 yards and then disgustedly tells the admiring Chico, "I was aiming for the horse!" He's a *perfectionist*.

The plot is that they are essentially losers - out-of-work gunmen, outcasts, superfluous - who come together in a noble cause and win a victory over the bandits and negative patterns. Lee overcomes cowardice, Vin learns to care about others, Chris keeps the contract though the job is more dangerous than he thought. It shows us that we all can transform. We all can be heroes. We are magnificent, but we won't know it until we ride off to battle…the only real battle…the battle with ourselves.

PART II
POPPING YOUR
PATTERNS

CHAPTER FOUR:
Identifying Your Patterns

"You should examine yourself daily. If you find faults,
you should correct them. When you find none,
you should try even harder."
- Israel Zangwill

We know by now that it is vital to look at ourselves in order to grow, but looking at ourselves is one of the most difficult challenges human beings can face. It's not always possible to do it by ourselves. Sometimes we need to enlist the help of a professional or wise friend.

I worked alongside Ivan, a brilliant Russian prison psychiatrist. At an IDTT, which is a meeting of psychologist, psychiatrist, correctional counselor, and inmate, Ivan responded to an inmate's request for therapy, "You want therapy? I tell you what is therapy. He" - pointing at me - "holds up mirror to you, and you look in mirror. That is therapy!"

The Pattern Identification and Reduction Therapy™ method is all about truth-telling and accountability: being honest with yourself about your patterns and accepting responsibility for everything you do. It's about having the courage to look in the mirror. It's about telling on yourself, for your own good. And the only way you can do this effectively is if you *observe*, rather than *judge*, yourself for having those patterns.

Open Your Eyes and Tell Me What You See

Before we get started identifying your patterns, I want you to try a little experiment. Look at whoever else is in the room with you and write down exactly what you see. If no one is in the room, imagine a friend or family member, and write down what you see in your mind's eye.

When I give this exercise to clients, they usually write, "I see my Uncle Rob, and he's a very loud guy, who probably drinks a lot 'cause he wants attention."

Hold on! That's not the assignment. Tell me what you *see* and not what you think or believe to be true about the person. This is an exercise in observation.

Remember Sherlock Holmes, the great fictional British detective? He was a master of observation. Holmes would glance at a man, turn to his sidekick, Dr. Watson, and proclaim, "Watson, that fellow has recently spent months in India hunting elephants, and lost his right pinkie finger in a shooting accident. He is married with two sons, and a successful stockbroker with a summer home in the Isle of Wight."

How could he know that? Because Holmes was a keen observer of that which is visible. To recognize patterns, you need only open your eyes and look around.

> "The world is full of obvious
> things which nobody
> by any chance ever observes."
> - Sherlock Holmes in *The Hound
> of the Baskervilles*

In a therapy group, I asked for a volunteer willing to be observed by the other clients. Jimmy raised his hand. I had him stand in front of the group and asked them for their observations.

"Jimmy is wearing a blue T-shirt, jeans, sneakers, a watch, and looks normal."

I wanted more details:

- Were his sneakers clean or dirty?
- What color was his watch?
- Did he have facial hair?
- What sort of hairstyle?

I asked the group members for more. They told me:

- Short grey hair
- Slim build
- Casually dressed
- Neat and clean
- Good hygiene
- Wedding ring
- Smiles a lot
- Tanned
- Probably 55 years old, but looks 45

I interviewed Jimmy for about five minutes, chatting casually about this and that, then checked back with the group for further observations. Here's what they added to their list after having listened to Jimmy's speech:

- Self-assured
- Bright
- Likes outdoor activities
- Talks about his family a lot, particularly his kids

- Sat calmly, no fidgeting
- Looked away when I asked about his father, who committed suicide 10 years ago

At that point, I asked the group what they deduced about Jimmy, based on what they'd seen and heard:

- A good guy, loves his family
- Takes care of himself
- Bright, educated, alert
- Still in pain over his father's death
- Not hung up on money or material things
- Had he really made peace with his father's suicide?
- Did he have suicidal or dark thoughts, too?
- Was the self-confidence a veneer? A mask? Or was he really okay with himself?

All of these deductions flowed from *what was visible* to the group members.

For the fun of it, next time you meet someone check out their shoes. That's all. Just their shoes. Observe the shoes closely and see what they say about the person. Are they plain or colorful? Squeaky clean, polished, or dusty? Stylish or old? Comfortable or stiff? Expensive or inexpensive?

You'd be surprised at what you can learn from study-ing a person's footwear. Just imagine what you can learn by paying careful attention to their clothing, grooming, hairstyle, walk, talk, body movements, and posture!

Observation, Not Judgment

I often conduct a group called "Strengths and Weaknesses." It's a simple, but intriguing exercise. Everyone in the group writes down the strengths and weaknesses of everyone else in the group so that each person gets to hear an honest appraisal of themselves. At the outset of one Strengths and Weaknesses group, a client warned me, "I don't want to judge anybody, or be judged." I replied, "This isn't judging. Judging is what *you* do. I'm observing. And observation means neutrality and *no* judgment."

We sometimes confuse observation with judgment. They are two totally different creatures. Judgment involves criticism, value differences, and negative emo-tion, often anger or fear. Think of the phrase, "Sitting in judgment on someone."

If I'm sitting in judgment on you, I'm determining right or wrong, and I more than likely have strong emo-tions about it, too. You ask, "Well, isn't it *wrong* for a guy to molest a little kid? Shouldn't we *judge* him as wrong?" True, it's a terrible and devastating crime. But if I'm enraged by it, and want to hurt or destroy the guy, we're both in trouble. In the words of Mahatma Gandhi, "An eye for an eye makes the whole world blind." What I could say is this: "He did something against the social code. He harmed a child. We're going to punish him for that."

When I judge, I am consumed by rage, and that is not helpful to anyone. A scientist studying a cell doesn't get red faced and yell, "Damn that cell! He's always acting stupid!" He merely observes and takes appropriate action. When you do 12-step work with a sponsor and share your character defects in Step Four, your sponsor is not supposed to say, "Oh, my God, Susan, you did what? You snorted cocaine while fooling around with your neighbor on a Ferris wheel ride? Shame on you, you little slut!" A good sponsor, like a rabbi, priest, or therapist, will listen to you and feel compassion. The sponsor helps you make sense of your actions, and not judge them.

Here's a cute joke my wife told me concerning the power of observation.

A young couple was in the Arizona desert, and the husband was talking about the amazing tracking abilities of the Native Americans. Up ahead, he saw an old Native-American man with white, braided hair and a headband, lying on the road, ear to the ground, palms flat on the pavement.

The old man looked up at the young couple and said, "White Dodge van. Man with red hair and woman with brown hair in front seats. Three noisy children, watching television in the backseat. Big, golden dog, happy, wagging tail."

"This is incredible," said the husband. "They're coming down the road?"

"No," said the old man, "just ran me over."

Seven Techniques for Identifying Your Patterns

We've established the importance of observation in spotting negative patterns, but how can we observe ourselves? The following techniques can be used to discover your patterns. But first you must give yourself *permission* to see your patterns. We move past resistance to the truth by reminding ourselves of these immortal words from the

Bible: "Ye shall know the truth, and the truth shall make you free" [John 8:32].

The truth may be painful, but it is also liberating and this is what we are aiming for – transformation and freedom.

Technique 1:
Look at Your Parents' Patterns

You might start by observing your parents. It's very likely that their patterns reflect at least some of yours. As my good friend Big Mike used to say back in Brooklyn, "The leaf doesn't fall far from the tree."

I asked my client, Jerry, to tell me all of his parents' negative traits, which I listed on a white board under the headings "Father" and "Mother." Father included "Know-it-all, thinks too much, worrier, cheap." Mother's traits were "Hyperactive, intrusive, bossy."

I asked him for their positive traits. Father's were "Good person, different interests, intellectual." Mother's were "Loving, high achiever, determined."

I asked Jerry, "How are you like them? Do you have some or most of those qualities?" The answer was, "Most."

Do we inherit our parents' qualities? Do we learn them at their knees? Or both?

In psychology, we refer to this as the "nature versus nurture" argument. In other words, what is it we are born with (nature) and what did we learn from others (nurture)?

It's not always possible to know, and perhaps in the long run it doesn't matter very much. But I do know that taking a hard look at our parents will often tell us a lot about ourselves.

Take a few minutes now to list your parents' strengths and weaknesses.

One side benefit of this exercise is coming to the realization that, despite our similarities, we are not our parents and we don't have to continue upholding the patterns they have handed down to us, if only we decide to make a different choice.

I was driving along the 101 freeway a few years ago on a beautiful spring morning, with shafts of brilliant sunlight piercing dark clouds. I wasn't thinking of much of anything when the thought came to me, unbidden, "I am not anxious."

This may not sound like a very profound thought, but it was powerful to me. I come from a long line of worriers. I'm convinced that an early Neanderthal Kadish turned to another Neanderthal Kadish and said, "I'm nervous. How about you, Al?"

I grew up in a family of ulcers, tensions, headaches, frazzled nerves, and occasional hysterical outbursts. This was normal for us. I developed my own pattern of inner anxiety (and sometimes outer anxiety), reacting to situations with fear and worry.

As I got older, the fear lessened a bit, but it still dominated my life. Years of therapy, coaching, introspection, and a commitment to change began to shift me, leading to that moment on the freeway, a true "aha!" moment, as if a shaft of sunlight had pierced my soul: *I wasn't like my family.*

I checked myself, as if discovering me for the first time, and realized, "I'm not nervous." In fact, I had never been nervous. Or more accurately, I had assumed a role, a persona, a duty, a way of looking at the world that had nothing to do with my true nature or temperament.

This was a monumental learning for me, and from it I developed my mantra: *You are who you say you are.*

I had told myself throughout my entire life that I was anxious, without really checking to see if it were true. As I looked deeply, I discovered that I had the choice of maintaining or losing my parents' patterns. I chose to lessen the anxiety pattern.

You are who you say you are

Here's an additional exercise to help you begin to break free of your parents' patterns. Make a simple list of your likes and dislikes: chocolate ice cream, old movies, and so on - whatever is true for you. How do they compare to your parents'? If you can see that your likes and dislikes are different from theirs, then you can see that you are you and they are them.

Technique 2: Observe Your Thoughts & Beliefs

As a child you developed beliefs and these became a part of the fabric of your thinking and approach to life. You are probably unaware of those beliefs because they are so ingrained in you.

Here's an interesting exercise: for the next 24 hours, write down as many thoughts as you can. These can be as simple as, "I should go to the store," "I hope Howard remembers to call me," or as meaningful as, "They say there's a God, but I'm not sure." Or, your thoughts may be dark and sinister. "I'd like to kill that son-of-a-bitch," "If there weren't laws against it, I'd take that woman right now, right here." Jot down what you truly think and feel. Do not judge your thoughts, only record them. How else can you change beliefs unless and until you first know what they are?

Patterns may reveal themselves to you if you track your thoughts and emotions for a full day. What do you see in your belief system? What conclusions can you draw about yourself after neutrally observing your thoughts?

Let me present an example of how to track your thoughts and feelings. It comes from Steve, a 28-year-old blue-collar worker from Colorado with a methamphetamine habit.

"Hope I get that job."

"My father is a jerk, but I still love him."

"Wonder if Sherrie is gonna call soon. I love that woman."

"I've got to pee bad."

"I should really visit Mom's grave."

"Every time I think of my father, I get angry all over again."

"I'll spit on Dad's grave when he dies."

"It's almost break time - I need a smoke."

"Sherrie still hasn't called, and I'm getting a little worried."

"Blue bird - beautiful - I love animals."

"My boss wants me back from break. Can't stand when he yells at me in front of the other guys."

Do you see the many themes and patterns?

- love and hate towards father
- guilt ("should" visit mother)
- anxiety ("Sherrie still hasn't called," "hope I get that job")
- humiliation ("yells at me in front of the others")

Everyone has worries about jobs and relationships. But notice that certain emotions or thinking patterns come up frequently for Steve. Chances are that if we read his 24-hour diary there'd be plenty more anger, guilt, and anxiety.

Here are some excerpts from Hillary's 24-hour diary:

"This is a stupid assignment."

"My hair is messed up today."

"I love Joey, he always comes through for me, no one else does."

"I'm wasting my time at this job, I want to quit."

"SCREW this job!"

"When my roommate gets home, I'm gonna tell her I'm moving out next week."

Hillary's patterns are evident, don't you think?

- negativity (about assignment, hair, job, roommate)

- defeatism (quitting job, giving up)
- mistrust (of everyone but Joey)

We have the picture of a hopeless, depressive, and injured person, who is probably sullen much of the time. And that's after reading only six lines from her diary!

What are your beliefs? Do you know? Write down the following topic headings on separate sheets of paper:

- Sex
- Relationship
- Religion
- Family
- Friendship
- Work
- Parents

You can add a few more, if you'd like:

- Politics
- Culture
- Neighbors
- Children
- Television
- Travel
- Education

Now, write down any and all beliefs you might have on these subjects.

Let's take the topic, "Children," and I'll show you how this assignment might look.

- ✓ I believe children are the future.
- ✓ I believe children should be silent.
- ✓ I believe if I ever have a child, I won't raise it the way my parents raised me.
- ✓ I believe children are much more important than adults.
- ✓ I believe children are a real pain.

Go ahead now, on a separate piece of paper, and write down as many beliefs as you can think of. Then come back to this spot in the book.

What is so important about our beliefs? They dictate our actions. The Buddha told his followers, "We are what we think. All that we are arises with our thoughts. With our thoughts, we make the world." *We are what we think.* We create our own world.

Here's a vivid example. I know plenty of hardcore gangbangers who believe that:

- ✓ The gang is everything.
- ✓ They are my family.

- ✓ I've got to be loyal to them.
- ✓ I will kill for my gang and our territory.
- ✓ I represent my gang to the fullest.
- ✓ The gang will never let me down.

They also believe in the concept of respect. If you disrespect a gangster, you will pay the price. They believe in an eye for an eye, and the power of violence. They believe that they could die in the service of the gang, and that's okay with them. See how powerful beliefs can be?

Actually, a lot of onetime gang members *did* believe that. They've since learned that gang buddies turn on them, are not always there for them, are not there for their families while they're in jail or prison - in short, that they will let you down.

These former gangsters now have new beliefs:

- ✓ Family is the most important thing.
- ✓ You've got to earn my trust.
- ✓ I'm loyal, but only up to a point.
- ✓ I'll do what I think is right, not what I'm told to do.

Here's another negative belief system: the guy who sees enemies everywhere. This is all too common on the prison yard. Now, on the one hand, it's true - there are enemies all over the place in prison. On the other hand, if you believe that everyone is against you, you will create enemies that weren't there to begin with. Or you'll isolate, avoid others, speak rarely if at all, and be tense and wary. Inwardly, you'll feel frightened, sad, upset, depressed, and lonely. When people meet you, you'll put out a bad vibe. They, in turn, may scowl at you, or even attack you.

> What you put out is
> what you get back

We hear a lot today about the Law of Attraction. This is perhaps the oldest spiritual law of all. What you reap, you sow. What you release, you receive. If you put out depression, you'll receive coldness and disinterest. If you put out a fear of being taken advantage of, you will receive nothing in turn.

If you believe, "People will hurt me," change your belief. Change it by writing down, saying out loud, and telling others, "Some people may hurt me some of the time." Better yet, how about something more positive, like, "Some people will help and befriend me some of the time." I think that's a true and realistic statement, even on a prison yard.

Be careful of your language and your self-talk. It reflects and exacerbates your negative patterns. Ask others to correct you if and when your speech is critical or self-damaging.

Technique 3: Become Aware of Projection

You can't change negative patterns until you've spotted them, but it isn't always so easy to spot them. What gets in the way? You! Or, more accurately, your need for self-importance.

Most of us do not want to recognize our own character defects, or our assets for that matter. From birth on, we've been doing everything in our power to avoid looking at them. We steer others away from noticing them, too. Some people say that looking in the mirror at ourselves is as easy as taking candy from a baby. Let me ask you this: have you ever tried taking candy from a baby?

Here's another way of figuring out your patterns, though you might not like the exercise. That's okay. Do it anyway.

Focus on someone you detest - a boss, a coworker, a guy you went to school with, your sister-in-law. Write down what you can't stand about that person. It might look something like the following, written by Tim.

My last boss, Wayne, was a jerk. There's no other word for him. Actually, there're plenty of other words for him, but that one suits him best. Anyways, Wayne had me work overtime twice. Once, I had to cancel dinner plans with my wife, and was she mad! Okay, fair enough. A week and a half later, he springs it on me again, last minute.

I tell him, "Wayne, that's not fair," and he gets all huffy and says, "Hey, life is not fair." But you know what really burns me the most? It's that he doesn't even say thank you. Nothing. Not a word.

What would you say Wayne's negative patterns were? He's rude, isn't he? Thoughtless, selfish, demanding, impolite, arrogant, bossy. It's not that difficult recognizing negative patterns in others. It's even easy to see where others lie, manipulate, bully, whine, complain, and blame. *It's much harder to see the patterns in ourselves.*

In this case, Tim easily recognized negative patterns in his boss. But he almost blew a gasket when I asked, "Tim, how are *you* like Wayne?" Trust me, Tim did not think he was *anything* like Wayne. But what he didn't realize is that other people act as our mirrors to show us disowned or unrecognized parts of ourselves.

In psychology, we call this "projection." Like a film projector, we cast our own traits out from ourselves and onto others like a movie screen and then think they are outside of us. This is much easier on the ego!

> If you hate a person, you hate something in him that is part of yourself. What isn't part of ourselves doesn't disturb us.
> - Herman Hesse

Before I was a psychologist, I managed a word processing center for a company in the San Fernando Valley. I couldn't stand my boss. Hated the guy. Wanted to throw him out a window. I was in graduate school at the time and had to do a projection assignment. I chose the boss as my subject.

I wrote and wrote about this guy - nearly a hundred double-spaced pages - judging him as arrogant, unfair, bossy and controlling (come to think of it, pretty much like Tim's boss, Wayne). The point of the assignment was to look and see if any of those qualities were also in *me*. They were. Yecch! I saw how, at certain times, I too was arrogant, unfair, and controlling. I recognized the patterns in my life by seeing them in my boss.

Recognize yourself by
looking into others

Positive projection, by the way, works in the same manner. We see in others traits or qualities that we admire; we may even idolize another person. We project onto them positive qualities that, in reality, they may or may not even possess. And we don't recognize that we too possess these qualities, at least to some degree. They may be dormant, not fully owned, or not fully developed, but they do exist. Otherwise, we would not have the ability to recognize or appreciate them in others.

The goal of working on ourselves is to become *whole* - first by owning all aspects of ourselves and then by diminishing the negative and enhancing the positive. Whenever you have strong feelings about someone else, whether negative or positive, check and see if projection is in play. Like I said, this can be a particularly difficult assignment, but the reward is a true and honest appraisal of yourself and a sure-footing based in reality from which to move forward.

Go, man, go!

Technique 4: Pay Attention to Your Feelings

We experience emotions all the time: anxiety, fear, sadness, joy, calm, worry, hurt, and more. However, it's possible that certain emotions come up *more frequently* for you than other emotions. Or that certain emotions come up with *greater intensity* than other emotions. This is a sure sign that a negative pattern is at work…perhaps several.

Barbara was a 42-year-old businesswoman from the Midwest who moped around in worn jeans and shapeless T-shirts, given to sighing and talking about how her ex-husband used her for her money. She complained about staff, and engaged in daily bouts of self-pity.

As Barbara paid attention to the constant emotions of sadness and depression, and we continually pointed out her negative patterns, she developed greater insight into where those patterns came from and how they manifested themselves. In her case, as with many clients, it stemmed from abuse and neglect in her childhood.

Barbara had been bullied by older siblings, ignored by her father, and mistreated by her cold mother. Barbara became a victim, perpetually disappointed in others. Eventually, with our assistance, she was able to diminish these patterns. But the starting point was her growing awareness of the emotions of sadness and depression, which occurred frequently and intensely.

Is there an emotion you experience often or intensely? Do the following brief exercise.

Ask yourself:

"What emotion do I frequently feel?"

"Why do I feel it?"

"What is it I gain from continuing to feel that way?"

Here is Stuart's response to this exercise:

I am sad. Nothing works out. I feel sad for myself a lot of the time.

What do I gain from this? Well, for one thing, people feel sorry for me. Which means they pay attention to me. Particularly girls. I make sure they know I have a lot of pain, and it sort of touches them or something.

One of Stuart's negative patterns, evident from this brief exercise, is self-pity. He doesn't just feel sad - he feels "sad for myself."

Focus in on the emotions that cause you constant stress. Try to figure out why they play havoc with your life. Do this exercise with as many emotions that trouble you, as many times as necessary. New material may emerge as you repeat the exercise.

Technique 5: Ask Others for Feedback

We are occasionally able to figure out our patterns, but not always. We can easily miss that which is too close to us. Try this: spread the fingers on your hand and place them over your eye, leaving the fingers open so that you can see through them. Now, imagine looking through your fingers, searching for your hand. You'd never see it, though it was touching your face!

Similarly, we sometimes fail to see our patterns because they are too close to us. However, other people may easily see our faults and virtues. As the Talmud says, "If one man says to thee, 'Thou art a donkey,' pay no heed. If two speak thus, purchase a saddle."

As I mentioned earlier, I occasionally conduct a monthly group called "Strengths and Weaknesses" where everyone in the group writes down the strengths and weaknesses of everyone else so that each person gets to hear an honest appraisal of themselves. The incredible thing about this exercise is how *consistent* the feedback is. Almost everyone tells Ed he's a whiner. They tell

Lainey that she's compassionate but takes better care of others than herself. They all see Victor as putting on a phony face, pretending to be happy and relaxed all the time.

Just telling the truth doesn't sound like much, does it? And yet so few of our friends, family members, and colleagues are honest with us. Why not?

Because they:

1) don't want to hurt our feelings
2) are scared of our response (i.e., we might blow up at them)
3) don't know how to be honest
4) don't see the need to be honest
5) don't want to spend time giving us feedback
6) feel weird being honest

I'm a firm believer in "rigorous honesty," a phrase I've been heard to use on occasion. Fernando, a former client, told me, "I've been doing that honesty thing a lot, with my boss, and my wife."

"What honesty thing?"

"You know. What you always talk about."

"What?"

"That retarded honesty."

While Fernando's mistake was politically incorrect, there was a core of truth to his slip. Honesty can feel awkward and uncomfortable. It's a difficult and unwieldy process for most of us.

While a therapy group is an ideal setting to practice asking for feedback, you don't need a group to do it. Here's what you can do instead: ask ten friends, acquaintances, coworkers, and relatives to write down your strengths and weaknesses in as few words as possible - no more than a paragraph - via email or a typed or handwritten note.

Why in writing? So that you can refer back to their *exact words*, which you'll have for posterity. Get a good mix of feedback givers...people who have known you forever and some who hardly know you at all.

Tom, a 47-year-old mortgage banker, used this technique, and here are some of the responses he received:

- "Tom, you get frustrated very easily."
- "Anger, dude!"
- "You are a wonderful guy, Tom. I've always thought so. But you do seem to lose your temper easily."
- "Dad, you yell too much and it scares me."

The emerging theme is *anger*. Tom appears to others as a volatile guy, easily agitated, and frightening to be around. You never know when he will blow.

Does this negative pattern mess up his relationships? You bet. People lie to him, placate him, and avoid him... and he doesn't even know it half the time. Other people with anger issues pick fights with him. Anxious people run away from him.

I like the "Ask Others" technique because it shows you your strengths, too. As I will continue to point out, we *all* have strengths, though we don't always see, or acknowledge, them. You already know my response when a client says to me, "I don't have any good points," I respond, "Stop lying to me." It plays out like this:

Them: (defensive)	I'm not lying to you!
Me:	Yes, you are.
Them: (stubborn)	Nothing about me is good.
Me:	Nothing?
Them:	No.
Me:	Like I said - you're lying to me. (beat) What if your best friend in the world were here? What would he/she say about you?
Them:	Well...that I'm a loyal person and I care about other people.

Me:	So there are some good things about you?
Them: (grudgingly)	Some.

By the time I'm done, the client will have admitted to at least three or four strengths.

It's interesting to me that human beings are often more willing to see their weaknesses than their strengths, though you'd think it'd be the other way around. I suspect it often has to do with the fear of success, feelings of shame, or a pattern of feeling guilty and undeserving.

I can't tell you how many clients I've counseled who were more willing to hold themselves back than push themselves forward. Why? Because they didn't want to appear immodest or arrogant. Our society tells us not to be vain or proud, though ironically, all of us are vain and proud. Remember how self-importance dominates our lives?

More importantly, we don't want to stand out. It's back to the Tall Sunflower Syndrome. "Don't be visible," we are warned. "Be small and unnoticed, and you will survive." Few people want to stand out and be targeted by the mob's envy. We don't want to be ostracized, gossiped about, or excluded from the group. So we do what we can to fit in and be accepted. *But at the price of not living up to our potential.*

I say enjoy your strengths. Be who you are. Wise, nerdy, adventurous, quiet, shy, heartfelt, capable, industrious, brilliant. *Just be you.*

President Harry Truman was a very earthy Midwestern guy, at all times true to his own character. When his daughter, Margaret, would have dates pick her up at the White House, Truman would show the boys around. He'd say, "See these roses? Know why they're so beautiful? Cow manure. That's the only damn thing to make a great garden."

One night Margaret said to Mrs. Truman, "Mother, don't you think we can get father to say something besides 'manure.' Can't he say 'fertilizer'?" Mrs. Truman shook her head sadly and said, "Margaret, do you know how long it took me to get him to say manure?"

> Be who you are and say what you feel,
> because those who mind don't matter
> and those who matter don't mind.
> – Dr. Seuss

Let's return to Tom for a moment, and read what his friends and family wrote about his strengths.

- "Tom, you are extremely intelligent!"
- "One funny dude!"
- "Tom, I really appreciate your loyalty and dedication to your friends, family, and employees."
- "Dad, I love your sense of humor and how you always protect me."

Tom has a whole range of strengths:
- humorous
- loyal
- dedicated
- intelligent
- protective

What are your strengths? Are you caring? Loyal? Strong? Purposeful?

A late-19th-century British socialite was asked which Prime Minister she enjoyed more as a dinner companion, Gladstone or Disraeli. She replied, "After sitting next to Mr. Gladstone at dinner, I thought he was the greatest person in England. But after sitting next to Mr. Disraeli, I thought *I* was the greatest person in England."

Maybe you, like Disraeli, are adept at making others feel worthwhile. You are a good listener, which is quite

a gift. Don't be ashamed or too modest to list your successes, accomplishments, and strengths from a detached
viewpoint. This is a good thing!

Technique 6: Make Time for Contemplation (a.k.a. Self-Reflection)

We don't often stop and reflect on our lives, beliefs, and
actions. It's not the nature of our fast-paced society. But
taking time to contemplate is perhaps the single most
important component of change. We can't change if we
don't ever evaluate what we're doing.

Contemplation is easy to do. It doesn't have to be
anything fancy. No need for formal meditation practice,
instruction, or expensive equipment. Simply get comfortable in a chair or on a couch, with or without soft
music. Whatever works for you. The key is to relax, let
your mind drift or go blank, and when you're ready,
think about your life. What is working? What isn't
working?

Nathaniel Branden, the noted psychologist touted
as the "Father of Self-Esteem," phrases it this way.
In his book *Taking Responsibility* he writes that each
morning when he wakes, he asks himself two questions: "What's good in my life?" and "What needs to

be done?" The first question keeps us focused on what we have to be grateful for in our lives, reminds us of the successes we have to build on, and creates the kind of uplifting feelings that motivate us to take positive action. Which leads into his second question. We can evaluate our life and look for the things that are not working so well and brainstorm solutions on how to improve the situation. I agree with Dr. Branden that this is a recipe for happiness.

Looking on the positive side, you may feel grateful that you have a roof over your head, a decent job, a car that runs okay. If you have none of these things, you may have to look a little harder, but there *is* something. Perhaps it's that you have the eyes to read these words or someone who is kind enough to read it aloud to you. Start with something positive in your life. There *is* something, I know it! Find it.

On the negative side, you may think of your failed marriage, difficulties with parents, and dull career. With regard to your thoughts and emotions, you may feel a constant sense of being worthless or worry that others will see you as the incompetent, idiotic mess you really are. Let the negative thoughts and emotions surface. You may get images, possibly of disturbing or sad events, such as the time you fell off your bicycle and no parent was around to take care of you, or doing poorly in college, dropping out, and feeling like a total failure.

Write down these pictures, scenes, or thoughts. They are indications of negative patterns, such as self-pity, self-loathing, fearfulness, mistrust, and so on. Explore these on paper, asking yourself questions about these pictures or beliefs. You may also want to seek the guidance of a counselor in interpreting and working with this material.

Think of a scene from your childhood that excited, disturbed, elated, entranced, upset, tickled, frightened, mortified, or amused you. What was the emotion you experienced at that time? What was the dominant thought you experienced at that time? If you look at the negative patterns listed in Chapter 3, which pattern(s) best describe this scene?

Technique 7: Document Your Dreams

Dreaming is similar to contemplation. As you probably know, we dream every night, though many people do not recall their dreams, claiming, "I don't dream." The truth is they do. Without REM stage sleep, we'd die. For many people, practicing jotting down dreams upon awakening will develop the ability to recall dreams. Write down the dreams you remember, and pay attention to themes that emerge: certain emotions, events, or people. These may be of significance to you.

Julie Ann notices that she keeps dreaming about Dave, her former fiancé. In real life, they broke up when he claimed he wasn't ready for marriage. Dave then turned around and married another woman. In her dreams, Julie Ann is always angry at Dave, and often hits, or even kills, him. She feels guilty for these dream emotions/actions and wants to hurt herself.

Her perception of Dave as a betrayer triggers her negative thoughts and feelings of being abandoned ("He left me"), of feeling incompetent ("How come every-one else can get a husband, but not me?"), and worth-less ("His wife is a lot prettier, plus I'm gaining a little weight these days"). Julie Ann's dreams can be con-strued as upsetting and vexing or as helpful indicators of the patterns that exist inside of her and that are crying out for correction.

Document your dreams. Observe the themes, emo-tions, and thoughts that come through, and spend some time thinking about what they may mean. Make notes about the patterns that seem to be emerging. I highly recommend keeping a dream journal next to your bed and writing your dreams down as soon as you awaken.

Otherwise, they can slip away as you move into your day.

Recognizing patterns calls for willingness and rigorous honesty. To be honest with yourself is to be courageous. Allow others to help you by asking them to point out your patterns. Simply listen to what they say, without justification or defense. I encourage you to take notes, or have them write down their assessment of you. Contemplate their words. Look for the truth of their observations. Look inside yourself. Your dreams, thoughts, beliefs, and musings will point out your patterns to you.

Who Else Can Point Out Your Patterns?

If you have tried each of these techniques and still do not feel you have a grasp on what some of your patterns are, you may want to seek help in figuring them out. Who else can point out your patterns to you? The short answer is anyone.

Ideally, however, this would be a therapist, 12-step sponsor, or pastoral counselor, but even a close friend could give you an opinion regarding your negative (and positive) patterns of thought, emotion, and behavior.

Keep in mind that not every therapist points out patterns in a straightforward way. Some therapists believe in taking a lot of time before telling the client the truth. Their training and inclinations may lead them to feel that you must see these patterns on your own. This is not a wrong approach; it's simply a different approach. If you prefer a "Brooklyn approach," work with a therapist who operates that way.

Sadly, some therapists don't ever see the truth. They may be gentle, kind, and well-intentioned, but you'll never get anywhere with them. Your life will remain the same: crummy relationships, job loss, and drug use. Seek a counselor who has the insight, guts, and integrity to tell you the truth.

CHAPTER FIVE:
Setting the Stage

We're getting close now. This chapter will set the stage for popping your patterns. But, as with any important task, before we tackle the problem, we need to get in the right frame of mind. So, prior to my giving you specific actions to pop your patterns, we need to talk about a few key components that will assist you in your efforts to change.

Motivation

We all want to change, or at least we say we do. But change requires motivation. We need a *reason* to change - a purpose, inducement, or incentive.

I can ask 5-year-old Willie to clean up his room, but we all know that offering him an ice cream bar or a video game will most likely amp up his desire to do what I ask of him. He has a real reason to take action.

Let me share an email sent to me by Herb, a businessman from San Francisco, who wrestled with a pattern of avoidance - running away from people or situations that angered or upset him.

Back in July of 2007, I was recovering from opiate and cocaine dependence. In one of my group sessions with Dr. Seth Kadish, I was confronted by two ladies whom I'd become very close with during the prior two weeks to coming to treatment. As I sat in the group session listening to what was being said about my being selfish, sarcastic, and not coming clean with all of my feelings and emotions about my situation with my wife, I had the sense that I was under attack. I remember feeing that as soon as this session was over, I would never talk or associate with these ladies again.

This had been a normal response for me all of my life. I would see the comments being made as harsh, hurting criticisms, and that THEY don't like me! I would naturally write them off and stay away.

After the session, I went to the restroom and looked in the mirror. I had remembered a previous session with Dr. Kadish where he had brought to my attention the fact that I had an opportunity to look at things differently, that maybe people say things to me and about me not to hurt me, but they say what they say out of genuine love and concern for me.

I was able to leave the restroom with a feeling of love from these two ladies. I showed up in their presence with that attitude, and felt very grateful that Dr. Kadish had pointed that pattern of mine out to me. It allowed me to change the course of my relationship with these two ladies for the remainder of my stay in treatment.

Herb gives me credit, and that is kind of him. However, if he did not confront himself - to literally look in the mirror - he would never have popped his pattern of avoidance.

Herb had a willingness to do it differently. He was serious about ridding himself of drug-taking, and even more serious about improving the relationships with the people in his life. He was *motivated*.

It's important to look at what motivates your desire to pop your patterns. The motivator may be small or large, trivial or powerful. Perhaps you just want to feel better about yourself, or to represent yourself in a more favorable light with others. Or maybe you want to avoid some serious consequence, like your spouse leaving you over an infidelity or facing jail time if you lose your temper and hit someone again.

Take a moment, and think of a negative pattern you'd like to change, something about yourself that isn't clicking and is causing you internal or external problems. Now, write down all the reasons you want to change this habit.

It could look like this, courtesy of Johnny:

I get red-faced easily. I seem to feel some kind of - I don't know - shame or guilt all the time. Like when I walk into a room at a party and I think everyone is staring at me and judging me. I just want to run away, or throw up. Sometimes I make a dash for the bar, and grab the biggest drink I can find.

The patterns are self-consciousness and embarrassment. Why does Johnny want to change? He tells me:

"I hate feeling like an idiot."

"I am envious of my brother - he's so self-confident."

"I'm angry at everyone who makes it look so easy."

How do you like those motivators? Hatred, envy, and anger. Not pretty, but certainly effective!

We're human beings. We're messy. Our motivations are oftentimes quite shoddy. Again, that's okay. No self-beating allowed here. I'd rather have lousy and useful motivators than sweet-sounding, useless ones.

The fictional Jamie Lou Johnson of Smithtown, Alabama, is a contestant in the Miss America pageant. She's blonde, sexy, and creamy. The judge asks Jamie Lou why she wants to win the title of Miss America. She replies, "I really want to help stop disease and starvation in Africa."

Have you ever heard such crap in your life? We all know it's ridiculous. Wouldn't it be a much more interesting show if she shared her real reasons for wanting to be Miss America?

"I want to meet a good-looking guy and have kids."

"I want money to open up my own business."

"I just want to get out of my home state, head to L.A., buy a fast car, and party."

"I don't want it at all - my mother wants it."

Are these motivators wrong? Shallow? Or merely human?

By the way, here's how I know that Miss America's altruistic responses are a joke: how many of the contestants who want to stop world hunger hop on a plane to Africa and devote their lives to helping the starved and diseased when the contest is over? I don't mean to say that they should. But please don't try to convince me that they care much about those causes. We all know that they are giving the pat answers they are supposed to give.

Don't judge your motivators. To the contrary, be honest with yourself. Start by acknowledging the truth of your thoughts and feelings. As my dad used to say, "Son, you can bullshit the world, but don't bullshit yourself."

Motivations may be genuinely pure, spiritual, altruistic - good for you! But remember our focus is on changing negative patterns that are keeping you from getting what you want in life. Let's utilize any motivators that are effective.

An analogy: I've got to escape from a 1,200-lb. grizzly bear. It's fast and furious, and coming right at me. I'm looking around for a way to get away. I'd love a brand-new Lexus sedan or a Harley-Davidson motorcycle, but all I see is a beat-up old bicycle with the paint chipping off it and a dented front fender.

Me, I'm jumping on it and getting out of there. You can wait for the limousine, if you like.

Now you try it.

List a negative pattern you want to work with and ask yourself, "Why do I want to change?"

The Importance of Commitment

Big Mike told me a story long ago that I still remember. When he and our friend Johnny D. were struggling young actors in New York, they took a job as bouncers at a well-known Times Square nightclub. Mike was tough, but John was even tougher. One night some drunken guys caused trouble and Mike and John threw them out. The guys came back later. One of them held a long, sharp knife in his hand. Without a pause, John walked into the guy and took the knife away, grabbing the blade in his bare hand. John was bleeding all over the place. As Mike told me, "Some guys think they're tough and some guys are tough. But John is *willing*."

To be willing is to be committed. It's to be ready to take action. It means striding into danger and difficulty. It means being fearless and brave. Popping patterns requires bravery and commitment, which in the simplest of terms means giving and honoring your word. In order to succeed at ridding yourself of a negative pattern, you've got to make a commitment to do so.

In my work with drug addicts, I've seen that motivation is crucial. You don't just stop using drugs. You need a reason to stop. You also need a sobriety plan that includes specific action steps, such as, "Attend a 12-step meeting daily," "Call my sponsor each day," "Go to an intensive outpatient program three times per week." But you won't succeed at your plan unless you are committed to following it.

In *The Magnificent Seven*, there's a pivotal scene in which the heroes, fighting against terrible odds, contemplate pulling out of the village and abandoning the peasants they've sworn to protect. When some of the gunmen speak persuasively in favor of quitting, Chris, the leader (Yul Brynner) responds, "You forget one thing. We took a contract."

"It's not the kind courts enforce."

"That's just the kind you've got to keep."

I've always been struck by the force of those words. They remind me of the Talmudic saying, "To break an oral agreement which is not legally binding is morally wrong."

In my own life, a promise given to an inmate - a man despised by society - is more sacred to me than a promise made to just about anyone else. This guy has no way to make me keep my promise. It's a matter of honor for me to keep my word to him.

> Don Miguel Ruiz, writes in *The Four Agreements*: When you are impeccable with your word, you feel good; you feel happy and at peace. You can transcend the dream of hell just by making the agreement to be impeccable with your word. Be impeccable with your word. Speak with integrity. Say only what you mean. Avoid using the word to speak

against yourself or to gossip about others. Use the power of your word in the direction of truth and love.

Are you impeccable with your word? Or, in Brooklyn terms, are you a bullshit artist - a "kidder"? "Kidders" always have excuses for why they can't do something. Everyone knows that their word is meaningless. "I'll get that to you tomorrow, I promise." "Don't worry, I'll take care of it." Yeah, sure, right.

How do you develop your impeccability? You learned to walk by using baby steps. You learned to lift heavy weights by first lifting lighter weights. It's the same with commitment. Before you commit to something difficult, such as erasing your self-pity or conquering your anger, commit to small, doable tasks.

This could look like:
- make my bed every morning
- floss my teeth once a day
- call Grandma once a week
- drive a bit slower
- reduce salty snacks

In other words, *start somewhere, with something!* And stick to it. Keep your commitment to yourself.

This small step will begin a much larger transformation process that will dramatically improve your life. That's because when you achieve small commitments, you feel confident and empowered. You develop trust in yourself, and become more trustworthy to others. This affects the way you behave in the world.

Honoring your word and taking small, consistent positive actions will put you squarely on the road to a new and improved life.

One Word of Caution Here (In Case Your Pattern Happens to Be People-Pleasing)

Don't over-commit or say yes when you really mean no! In addition, say no when you don't want to do something. People often overlook the simplicity and power of "no." I'll always ask a client, "Would you like to participate in this exercise?" "Would you like to hear my feedback?" I love to hear a "Yes," but always accept a "No." I do not accept, "Maybe," "Well…," "Whatever," or a lukewarm, "Sure."

When I ran the word processing center years ago, I had an employee named Bill, a calm, quiet, and mild-mannered guy who had the curious habit of typing standing up. One day, Evelyn, a secretary, came into our department and asked me to buy a box of cookies to help support her son's Little League team. I fished out a couple of bucks and gave it to her. So did my coworkers, Janey and Ellen. When she asked Bill for a contribution, he quietly said, "No." Just like that.

You could have knocked me over with a feather! I wasn't very good at saying no at that time in my life, and I was horrified (and secretly envious) that he'd done so. I thought of all the times I really wanted to say no, but instead said yes. She asked him again, as if he were a bit slow, and he repeated, "No." He didn't explain nor were there any guilt-ridden excuses: "I'm short of money," "I just gave last week," "My kid is in the Little League, too." He simply smiled at her, calm as could be, and said, "No."

In that moment, I learned how powerful "No" was, and just how difficult it was for me to say it.

I encourage you to say, "Yes!" to what you want, and "No" to what you don't. It will be a small step with a very big result.

Accepting Responsibility for Everything You Do

You want to do something great for yourself and makes leaps and bounds with your patterns? Accept responsibility for all of your actions. If you choose to walk into a building and a ceiling tile hits you in the head, say to yourself, "Well, I chose to walk into the building." It's a radical notion - and it probably flies in the face of your current belief, which says, "It's the builder's fault for putting up a defective ceiling." But it will move you forward in your life.

When I get stuck in a traffic jam, my self-talk is, "I chose to leave at this time and take this specific route." Rather than get caught in blame, I take responsibility for my decision and look for something constructive to do during that stalled drive rather than rage at and curse the traffic or the other drivers. I will ask myself if, spiritually, maybe I was supposed to be stuck here for some reason. Perhaps I would have had a car accident if I'd taken a different route home.

In addition, accept responsibility for all of your upsets. Let's say you're annoyed because you're watching TV, and along comes your brother, who switches from the movie you're watching to a football game. Rather than verbally attack him, or angrily switch the channel back, say to yourself, "I'm annoyed because Danny switched the TV station without asking me." Then, calmly tell Danny you were watching a movie, and discuss the situation with him.

The difference here is that you will first recognize your own state of emotions before reacting angrily to the event. Danny is not upset - *you* are. The upset is not his - it's yours! I'm not talking about being passive or rolling over like a dog. What I'm talking about is defeating patterns. And if one of your patterns is excessive anger, constant upset, and immature reactivity, you've got a problem. That will bleed into all areas of your life. How are you going to be calm and deal realistically with the world if you're always getting upset and blowing up at everybody?

Reframing for Success

Dr. Viktor Frankl was a Viennese psychiatrist who, in September 1942, was arrested, along with his wife, mother, father, and brother by the Gestapo and sent to the Theresienstadt concentration camp in Bohemia. Dr. Frankl became Prisoner No. 119104.

His entire family, with the exception of himself and one sister, was murdered by the Nazis. Frankl managed to survive the camp, and after the war, remarried and resumed his psychiatry and teaching duties. He also wrote a landmark book, *Man's Search for Meaning*, which has sold millions of copies, to date.

Frankl's book explained his views on human nature and survival in the concentration camp, as well as his system of logotherapy, a form of psychotherapy that looks at the importance of *meaning* in human life. Frankl believed that human beings always have a choice about how to act in the world. He surmised from his camp experience that every other freedom could be taken away from us except the freedom to choose how to view the events of our lives.

Reframing means to see the same picture, but in a different frame of your choosing. Frankl could have chosen to see nothing but misery and death, and yet he consciously noted bits of beauty in the harshest of environments. He chose to see his Nazi captors as flawed beings, many of whom were caught in a system, an evil machine, just like himself.

Years ago an elderly driver cut me off on the freeway. I didn't know why he cut me off, but I made up a story in my mind that he was no good. "That guy is a dirty bastard! He stinks." A friend innocuously pointed out to me that maybe the guy was having a medical emergency, or en route to see his daughter, who was giving birth to his first grandchild.

Light bulbs went off. Wow! Perhaps my assumption was all wrong. It's easy to fear and dislike an irritable old man, impatient to get to his destination and endangering my life, but not so easy to hate a man who is in dire need of a bathroom, having a heart attack or rushing off to see his elderly wife in the hospital emergency room.

Reframing is a valuable tool. Here's an example of how to use it in your daily life: your husband comes home from work in a bad mood. You decide that he is an angry, insulting jerk. What's your response? You slam his food on the table and retreat to the den to watch TV.

You could reframe the picture as follows: your husband comes home in an angry mood. You don't know why. You ask him what's going on. He tells you, "Nothing!" You ask again, and he confesses that he screwed up at work and he's convinced his boss is going to fire him. You calm him down, suggesting maybe it isn't so bad, but that he ought to talk to his boss as soon as possible.

What a difference the choice to see the situation in a different light makes!

In prison, inmate Rodriguez thinks inmate Contreras is "mad dogging" (staring) at him for no reason. Rodriguez interprets the stare as a threat. But what if he's wrong? Suppose that Contreras is developmentally disabled? Or thinks he recognizes Rodriguez from somewhere? What if Contreras is a daydreamer who's not even aware he stares at people? Rodriguez could end up in a beef with Contreras, maybe even slashing the guy's throat, and for no real reason. Contreras could be dead, and Rodriguez could pick up another charge, putting him in prison for life.

Be Vigilant Against Your Patterns

You need to know going into this process that you must be vigilant against your patterns. They are like addictions. In fact, they may even be chemical addictions. Studies have shown that emotional responses, such as anger, release chemicals in the brain, which we can actually become addicted to. Ever had the feeling that some people are just addicted to feeling bad? Like any addiction, though it's possible to free yourself from it, you should always be on guard against its return.

I gave up my cigarette habit years ago. Today, I don't want one, I wouldn't smoke one - but just to be safe, I won't even touch one. A silent and hidden temptation to smoke is always present and lurking somewhere deep inside of me. I'm honest with myself about it and I take precautions to keep myself straight.

This is true of our patterns, too. If you were addicted to anger, you would want to be very careful around angry feelings. If your pitfall was self-pity, you'd do well to be wary of situations which would trigger your self-pity.

Does this mean that we are never truly rid of patterns? Possibly. I do know that they are dangerous, and we must always be vigilant against their reappearance.

CHAPTER SIX:
Releasing Your Patterns

Releasing a negative pattern requires an action. Such an action is called an intervention. According to Webster's dictionary, to intervene is "come in or between so as to hinder or modify." It is our goal to erase or diminish negative thoughts, emotions, and behaviors by hindering or modifying them. In essence, we want to *interrupt* our negative, unproductive patterns and then redirect ourselves into more positive, productive ones.

If we don't do something to interrupt our patterns, they will linger on and on. It's Newton's First Law of Motion: "A body in motion will remain in motion unless acted upon by an unbalanced force." In other words, something will continue heading in the direction it's already in, until a force comes along and causes its course to change. Therefore, an intervention means *doing* something, and not just talking about it.

This is my big issue with talk, or insight, therapy. I am not opposed to it. To the contrary, I think it is a valuable part of the therapy process. Usually, though, it isn't enough to effect a true transformation, which requires *doing* something different. As they say, "Talk is cheap." Scrooge doesn't merely alter his thoughts about love and money - he takes action: he buys a huge turkey and has it delivered to the Cratchit family.

My client, Winny, complained that she and her mom argued every night on the phone.

"What do you guys argue about?" I asked.

"Everything. Anything."

"Do you want to stop arguing?"

"Yes, Seth!"

"Good. So when are you gonna talk to your mom next, Winny?"

"Tonight."

"All right. Here's what I want you to do. When you call your mom –"

Winny leaned forward, expectant.

" - stand on one foot."

"Huh? What?!"

"Stand on one foot."

"Why?"

"To do it differently. Now, if you really want to do it differently, talk to her in Chinese."

Winny laughed. "But I don't know Chinese!"

"Even better."

We must interrupt our patterns with actions. You must transform your negative thoughts and behaviors by replacing them with positive thoughts and positive behaviors. Such transformation is the result of interventions.

Often, making a change in the body can facilitate a shift in the mind and emotions. They trigger each other. It doesn't matter which one you start with and for many of us, it can be much easier to start with the physical. We can get to the belief later.

For example, David, a business owner, told me he wanted to be more spiritual. He wasn't really sure what he meant by that, but he knew it was a dimension that was lacking in his life. I recommended he start by being good to other people, and I asked him if he wanted to try it.

He said, "Well, what do you mean?"

I asked him, "How many employees do you have?"

"About 150," he replied.

I said, "And how many of them do you know by name?"

"A few."

I recommended that every day he go to the company cafeteria and sit at a table and talk to his employees.

"That's spirituality. That will get you on the track you want to be on. That's all you have to do. Do that for a month and then report back to me about how you feel. You don't have to save the world, just listen to your employees."

That small step moves his intention into the physical realm. Again, it's more important that he do that first and afterwards go back and look at the beliefs.

Every seasoned clinician has interventions that work well with clients. I've got a few of my own that I like very much. The following interventions were specifically chosen because you can do them on your own; they require little or no help from others. Each is designed to help you recognize and diminish your negative pattern.

The first two interventions involve writing, and are based in telling the truth. Without the truth, how can we recognize - and correct - our negative patterns? We tend not to examine the thoughts and emotions that we judge as ugly, wrong, bad. We let them go by without processing them. To process is to think, feel, and express, in spoken or written words.

I believe in getting under the surface of things. I'm perpetually interested in true thoughts and feelings - not what we're supposed to think and feel, but what we are really thinking and feeling.

Intervention #1: Keep an Honesty Book

Years ago, it occurred to me that one of my most steadfast patterns was lying. It wasn't so much that I was dishonest with others (though I was), it was more that I'd suppress my true thoughts and feelings to appease others. I didn't even know what my true thoughts and feelings were half the time.

What to do? I racked my brain until I came up with a simple solution. I'd create a notebook in which I'd write down my truth - I called it an "honesty book." Each sentence would begin, "The truth is…" and I'd write down how I *really* felt about God, violence, sex, people, myself, my family, the world around me. I wouldn't show the contents to anyone (and still haven't to this day). I wrote in it for several years, allowing myself the luxury of declaring my true thoughts and feelings, no holds barred.

If you are going to keep such a journal, make sure to put it in a very secure place, or even destroy it if and when you feel it's served its purpose. If anyone gets their hands on it, you are not runnin' for public office. Forgetaboutit!

Here are a few brief examples of how it might look.

"The truth is…I smiled at Cindy today but I was really angry at her and hid my feelings."

"The truth is…I sometimes feel happy but stop myself from laughing. I don't know why."

"The truth is…I love dogs and will one day buy a puppy."

"The truth is…chocolate is no good for me, and I make these fake promises to stop eating the stuff."

It feels good to be honest, doesn't it? Maybe a little scary, too, but I think what it really is is liberating. This is the beginning of true inner freedom.

Intervention #2: Break It Down

Take something that happened to you recently, an incident that rattled or disturbed you. It doesn't have to be anything big. In fact, it could have been a minor upset. Break it down. Look below the surface. What was really going on in your heart and mind at the time? Keep breaking it down until you can no longer "go below."

Let me give you an example: I was moderating a panel at a conference and one of the panelists, a well-known physician, was rambling on. Here were my true thoughts and emotions about the situation:

- I was anxious and worried that he'd never end.
- I was a little angry at the guy.
- "What kind of idiot is he? Doesn't he know to stop himself?"
- "What kind of idiot am I? I'm the moderator - I should stop him."
- "But if I'm rude to him, he'll hate me."
- "And the audience will hate me for being rude."
- "But if I don't stop him, I'll look weak."

See how one little episode created so much turbulence inside me? If you're wondering what I did with the blowhard guy, the answer is - nothing. I waited for a pause in his speech, and then guided the discussion back to the other panelists and audience members.

Internally, though, I did do something. I moved away from my anger and anxiety, and focused instead on the next audience question. I had little control over this guy. But what I could do was calm myself through positive self-talk: "All right, let it go. He'll stop at any moment, which is better than getting into a control battle with him, or embarrassing him."

Let's break down my thoughts even further.

Break It Down #1

The guy is talking too much, upstaging the other panelists, and I feel anxious.

- I am worried he'll dominate the panel.
  - If he does, the panelists and audience will lose respect for me.
    - If they lose respect for me, they will see me as weak and incompetent.
      - If I'm weak and incompetent, I'm no good.

Break It Down #2

The guy is talking too much, upstaging the other panelists, and I feel angry.

- He is challenging me.
  - …Humiliating me and disrespecting me in front of everyone.
    - I feel shame.

As you can see, the technique is simple: first I lay out the scenario, and include my feeling about it ("worried," "angry"). Then I look at the thoughts that are running parallel to the feeling. I do my damndest to get down to bedrock, and keep going below until I reach my innermost, truest, core thoughts and feelings. In a sense, I'm shining a light on my buried thoughts and feelings. Picture a cave explorer, wearing a helmet with a little flashlight built in. He slowly rappels down the rope, peers around, admiring the stalactites and stalagmites, and then descends deeper and deeper into the cave. He is exploring. He is discovering. So are you as you "go below," gaining insight into your negative patterns, uncovering the true thoughts and emotions that create and fuel them.

Let's look at one more example. Wallace got fired from his last job. He felt tremendous rage and couldn't process it. I had him do this exercise. Concerning his anger at his boss for firing him for weak performance, he wrote:

- I felt humiliated.
  - In my heart, I knew I was not very good at sales.
    - I felt incompetent.
    - I felt ashamed at being a failure.

What has happened recently that caused you some upset? What were the true thoughts and emotions you were experiencing? Break it down:

- Situation
- What you thought and felt
- Remember, keep going below!

Intervention #3: Swing the Pendulum (The Principle of Exaggeration)

Have you ever observed the movement of a pendulum? It swings all the way to the left and then to the right until, eventually, it winds up in the middle. Using exaggeration as an intervention works in much the same way. Think of the negative behavior as swinging all the way to one extreme. You want to exaggerate your newly learned positive behavior in the opposite direction until you arrive at a middle point.

Cindy, a young woman in my group, often interrupted me and her peers. She did it because she was anxious and worried that she would not be heard by the others. It was a very annoying pattern. To assist her in curbing the interruptions, I'd have her wait patiently, with hand raised, each time she wanted to speak. I'd often bide my time before calling on her. When I did call on her, she'd have to wait another three seconds - an eternity to her - before speaking to the group. The intervention was cal- culated to slow her down and to emphasize the power of listening. Interrupters don't listen - they are focused on what they want to say and how quickly they can say it, which makes it impossible to hear anyone else.

In another instance, I had shy Norman stand in front of the group on a regular basis to help him conquer his fear of being seen by others. This also decreased his negative patterns of self-consciousness and poor self-esteem.

I'm working with a young woman right now who tends to answer questions in a circular manner. Belinda never really gets to the point. She doesn't usually respond to the question I ask. I coach Belinda on two new behaviors.

1. Repeat what I've just said.
2. Answer me in as concise a manner as possible.

Properly executed, it goes something like this:

Me: "How are you feeling today?"

Her: "How am I feeling today? Good. A little bit of a headache, but otherwise okay."

Me: "Are your parents coming down for a family session?"

Her: "Are my parents coming down for a family session? I don't know yet. I'm waiting to hear back from them."

I worked with Neil, who was on the glum and negative side. Whenever I made a suggestion to him, he'd reply, "Yes, but…." You couldn't win with the guy. I called him "Mr. Yes But." He could be negative about anything.

Do you know people like that? You say, "Hey, you won a free trip to Hawaii!" and they reply, "Yes, but it rains a lot in Hawaii." You say, "Your new car is beautiful," and they reply, "Yes, but it uses too much gas." They find a reason to be unhappy about everything. Abraham Lincoln recognized this tendency in many human beings, and remarked, "Most folks are about as happy as they make up their minds to be."

Neil, on some deep level, had made up his mind to be unhappy and doubting. He had a series of beliefs about himself and the world that showed up in his pattern of negativity and oppositionalism. He had learned early on that he if he expected the worst, he'd never be disappointed in life. But now, as a middle-aged man, he expected the worst - and that's what he kept getting, day after day.

Are you a "Yes, but" person, too? If so, try something radical and different. Say "yes," wherever applicable.

The movie "Yes Man" is a great illustration of this concept. The main character (played by Jim Carrey) is negative and pessimistic in outlook until he attends a seminar led by a charismatic speaker who encourages the crowd to say yes in their lives. Jim Carrey takes this advice and becomes wildly successful in all areas of his life – work, finance, romance, friendship. (He does, however, need to learn to say no at times.).

In the early 1980s, I studied improv comedy in Manhattan. One of the basic techniques we were taught was to agree with our scene partner, no matter what they said. I might start a scene by saying to my partner, "Well, Mr. President, it seems that our war with Iceland is not going well." A good scene partner would immediately accept that reality, and give me an attitude or title in return, such as, "That's right, General Fenwick. We're doing poorly in Iceland. I want you to organize a Reindeer Brigade."

Inexperienced (or bad) improv performers would deny the other person's reality. I'd say, "Well, Mr. President, it seems that your war with Iceland is not going well." Then they'd reply, "I'm not the President. Stop calling me that!" Where do you go from there? Nowhere. You're done.

To repeat: if you're a "Yes, but" person, learn to say yes to others. Learn to say yes to life!

Whatever your pattern is, *do the opposite*! Push the pendulum *all the way* to the other side in order to arrive at a normal, or middle, point.

For example:

If you're tardy, don't just show up on time - *be early*.

If you're selfish, don't be less selfish - *be very generous*.

If you are anxious, don't be less anxious - *be extremely calm*.

Whatever your pattern is,
do the opposite

Over weeks and months, your exaggerated behavior will lead to a more fruitful and positive behavior.

Marcy could never get up on time. A good solution was for her to buy a loud alarm clock and set it for twenty minutes before breakfast. An even better solution was for her to set it an hour early. She followed the coaching ("Don't be on time, be early"), and soon developed the habit of being prompt to appointments.

Earlier in this book I spoke about Alice, who was convinced that other people did not like her. She was no good, and they did not care for her. When she asked me for advice, I told her to pretend that everyone liked her all the time.

"You mean lie?"

"Yep. Lie."

"But I'm an honest person. I don't like to lie."

"Really! Then why do you do it all the time?"

"I don't lie!"

"Yes you do. You say no one likes you."

"But no one does."

"What about me? Your cousin Stephen? Your brother Jeremy? Your roommate Nan?"

"Well…"

"Your lie can only be contradicted by another lie - that *everyone* likes you."

"That's two lies!"

"Which will lead you to the truth - that some people like you some of the time."

Pattern	Exaggerated Behavior
Rudeness	Gentlemanly:
	• Open doors for others
	• No profanity
	• Good table manners
Passive-aggressive	Assertiveness:
	• Write an honesty journal
	• Tell the other person the truth
	• No hidden resentments

Seduction	Asking for what you want:
	• No baby voice, sexual over-tones, cutesiness, innuendo
	• Ask in a normal voice
	• Be okay if you don't get what you want

Intervention #4: Reduce Negativity

An inmate once asked me, "Dr. K., how can I go from being depressed to not depressed?" "Jackson," I replied, "I don't know if you can go from being depressed to not depressed. But I'm confident you can go from depressed to *less* depressed."

You too can aim for a smaller goal - cutting down from 20 cigarettes a day to 18 cigarettes a day. Make commitments that are attainable. If you set the bar too high and fail, you'll only beat yourself up more, and indulge in the very behavior that you wanted to erase. Remember the alcoholic who fails at breaking the alcohol habit and, feeling bad, drinks more?

Take small steps to achieve your goals. You'll build confidence in yourself as you succeed. It's not always necessary to erase a negative pattern, but it is vital that you diminish it, a bit at a time.

Let's take the negative pattern of anxiety. You typically worry a lot, pace the floor, and share your fears and concerns with anyone who'll listen.

Let's have you choose any one of these behaviors, and commit to *reducing* it.

- Instead of pacing the floor for 10 minutes, pace for only 5.
- Instead of pacing the floor at all, practice deep breathing.
- Instead of pacing the floor, do the "Break It Down" intervention described earlier.

Let's do another one. This time, the pattern is guilt.

- Write down everything you feel guilty about.
- Add things to the list that are clearly not your fault, for example, the cancellation of your favorite TV show, the results of the presidential election, and so on.
- Decrease guilt by crossing out items on the list, starting with the ones that are clearly not your fault, telling yourself, "I am not responsible for this."

To reduce negativity, you can either increase positive thoughts and actions, or decrease negative thoughts and actions. For example:

- Say "Yes" at the beginning of 10 sentences a
  day:

Question: "Do you want to go to lunch?"

Answer: "Yes, I'd love to" or "Yes, I'd love to, but not today because I have an appointment. How about Thursday?"

- Reduce insulting or pessimistic statements to yourself, such as "I'm an idiot" or "It will never work out" from 20 times a day to 10 times a day.

I bet you could come up with five or ten more actions to reduce the negative pattern.

Intervention #5: Talk to the Mirror

Here's an exercise I did to break my pattern of low self-esteem, one of the most common and deep-rooted of all patterns. Look in the mirror and say aloud something you like about yourself, and then something you don't.

"I like my hair, but hate my chin."

"The chest is good, but the stomach's too flabby."

Take a neutral look at yourself, and determine what's good and what's not. Then figure out if you can improve the bad, or learn to accept it.

After you've completed a look at your physical self, ask yourself what you like, and don't like, about your personality.

"I like that I'm ambitious, but I'm often in an angry mood."

"I am very determined, but sometimes too stubborn."

It's the same principle at play. Enjoy what's working, and make a plan to change what is not working, but within your power to change. This is the essence of the 12-step serenity prayer.

> God grant me the serenity
> to accept the things I cannot change,
> the courage to change the things I can,
> and the wisdom to know the difference

Remember Dr. Branden's two questions: "What's good in my life? What needs to be done?" Taking this kind of proactive measure will improve your self-esteem and keep you moving forward in correcting a pattern. While it's not possible to change all physical defects, such as a missing limb or some medical conditions, personality defects are almost always subject to improvement.

Jack is a pleasant, affable former salesman who is now managing a sober living home. Everything about him is relaxed and easygoing. You may argue, "He will never be a very fiery guy - it's not his temperament." I disagree. His *passivity* can be changed. You can be easy-going, but also ambitious and proactive.

Anita is a quick-witted, intelligent investment banker, given to sarcasm and criticism. But she could be quick and bright without being hurtful to others. If she tells you, "I'm sarcastic, that's just the way I am," don't believe it! Quick and smart, yes - she was born with that kind of brain power and verbal ability. But sarcastic? Sorry. She's not stuck with it. Sarcasm can be unlearned and replaced with humor, kindness and playfulness.

Intervention #6: Practice Positive Self-Talk

Many books and articles have been written on the power of positive self-talk, but I'd be remiss if I didn't mention the topic here. Practicing positive self-talk is one of the great ways to combat negative thinking and behavior.

Our internal dialogue is habitual. The voice in our head drones on and on, providing a running commentary on ourselves and the world. If the self-talk is negative -

"I'm such an idiot, I hope they didn't see me do that, am I a moron!" - then the behaviors will be negative, too. It's vital that you correct your negative self-talk.

The very best way to stop negative thinking and self-talk is to start thinking and making positive statements. The reason is that you can't say something positive and negative at the same time. It's impossible! Likewise, our brain cannot hold a negative thought and a positive one at the same time. If we choose a positive thought, we are automatically choosing *not* to have a negative thought.

There are lots of ways to do this, including *affirmation*. Now, I'm no fan of flowery affirmation. Being a Brooklyn guy, I prefer short and to the point: "I'm a good man," "I care about people," "I'm nice looking." "I like me." However, it's your self-talk. You may love flowery! If so, try this one. "I am the loving essence of my soul's reflection." Do it any way you want, as long as it's believable to you.

I said earlier that you are who you say you are. But, let's temper this statement with Dirty Harry's (Clint Eastwood's) warning: "A man's got to know his limitations." If you're a high school dropout with a 92 IQ score, you can affirm, "I'm a brilliant guy" all you want, but the truth is that your intelligence is no great shakes. I can say, "I'm better looking than Brad Pitt," but that won't get me on the cover of *People* magazine. Find out who you are and affirm what is true about you. "I'm a bright guy" versus "I'm a genius." "I'm attractive" versus "I'm movie-star handsome." Let's keep it real!

Be vigilant about self-putdowns. There's no need for them. They're bad for you. Not only do they make you unhappy, they're impractical: they don't motivate you to take the kind of actions that will get you want you want in life. If you make a mistake, simply say, "That was a goof," and *not* "I'm a moron." You might even say, "I do some pretty dumb things sometimes," and laugh about it. That's an example of self-deprecating humor. But no serious putdowns, please.

In addition to talking to yourself in a loving manner, always accept compliments from others.

I've worked with numerous clients whose patterns of worthlessness, poor self-esteem, and self-loathing were positively impacted by this simple intervention. Accept compliments and do not *minimize* ("I'm an okay dancer…not that great…") or *deflect* ("I like to dance, but my brother, Ray, now he's a great dancer!").

Did you ever stop and think of the effect you have on others when you don't take in their compliment? In a sense, you're telling them they're dumb or crazy! It makes me mad when others don't accept my compliment. If I tell Rhonda she's extremely bright, and she minimizes, deflects, or denies, I feel frustrated. I may also feel crazy ("I thought Rhonda was smart, but maybe I'm wrong. Maybe I'm not that good a judge of character").

> Always accept compliments. It's easy.
> Just say, "Thanks."

I recommend the following exercise: read your list of strengths out loud once a day. When you do so, you'll be affirming your positive traits, engaging in positive self-talk, and improving self-esteem.

Build on your strengths and work on improving weaker areas. Draw on your successful experiences to prove to yourself that change is possible. Tell yourself, "I can do this. I *am* doing this!"

Intervention #7: Use Metaphors

It is very important to pay attention to the metaphors we use in our speech, as they have tremendous power. Read the following statements and consider what images they bring to mind:

- "I feel like the weight of the world is on my shoulders."
- "I'm drowning in a sea of garbage."
- "This project is killing me!"

Anthony Robbins, in *Awaken the Giant Within*, advises: "If you are feeling really bad about something, take a quick look at the metaphors you're using to describe how you are feeling, or why you are not progressing, or what is getting in the way." Pay attention to your words, inspect them and determine what's underneath them. Someone who says, "I have the weight of the world on my shoulders" is dealing with a feeling of overwhelm and may be negative or pessimistic in their views. They'll have physical symptoms such as feeling tired or not wanting to get out of bed.

To combat this, take an opposite action. For example, this person could buy feathers from the crafts store and put them on their shoulders, or perhaps get a pair of angel wings if they are more New Age inclined. Or they could place some kind of a weight on their shoulders and then knock or shake that off to demonstrate the removal of the weight they have been metaphorically carrying. Use this physical activity in conjunction with a new positive affirmation about the desired state.

One note of caution here: be careful not to state in your affirmation what you *don't* want. For example, you wouldn't want to say, "I no longer have the weight of the world on my shoulders." Yes, you are stating that you no longer have the problem, but in actuality you are still reinforcing the problem. The reason is that we are largely visual creatures. When we hear words, we convert them into images on the screen of our mind. But we can't visualize negatives such as "don't" or "no" or "no longer." Therefore, a much more effective affirmation for bringing about the positive feeling we are going for would be something like, "I feel completely limber and free," or "Life is easy and flowing."

Following are some examples of working with metaphors.

One of our clients, Peter, felt like he was walking on eggshells with his wife. Guess what we had him do? That's right - walk on eggshells. Instead of walking around them or lightly stepping on them, he stomped on 'em, and it felt good.

Sally talked to her therapist about jumping into new waters, and her therapist had her physicalize this goal by jumping into the pool.

Amber had a pattern of being defensive whenever her best friend pointed out any of her shortcomings. Exasperated, her friend threw his arms in the air and proclaimed, "You can lead a horse to water, but you can't make him drink." Amber had been working with me on her defensiveness and we had discussed the concept of metaphors. She recognized her friend's use of a metaphor and saw it as an opportunity to pop her pattern. Immediately following her friend's comment, Amber went to the kitchen, filled a glass with water, and proceeded to drink the whole thing, all the while affirming to herself that she was drinking in the feedback rather than defending against it.

In order to change, it is important to do different things...or do things in a different way.

A final story about working with metaphors.

Stanislau came to treatment to deal with a pain-killer addiction. He had been in a freak accident involving him and a friend tumbling down a flight of stairs. Stanislau had been hurt. His friend broke his neck and died.

They were not drunk or high at the time. They had been horsing around, and they slipped and fell.

Stanislau took pain pills for the back injury, and also to numb his terrible feelings of guilt. After all, he had murdered his friend...or so he believed. His peers tried to talk him out of his guilt. They rightly exclaimed, "It wasn't your fault, you didn't mean to hurt your friend." But Stanislau would not be budged. Whether intentional or not, he had caused his friend's death.

In his mind, he had spilled blood. With that in mind, I asked him if he were willing to give blood to atone for his deed.

Intrigued, he said, "How?"

"Couldn't be simpler. Go to your local Red Cross and donate blood."

"How often?"

"As often as it takes. Once, twice, a hundred times."

"Will that make the guilt go away, Dr. Seth?"

"It might. It will at least make it grow smaller, Stan."

Listen to your speech. You are describing your issues constantly in your daily language, whether you realize it or not. The good news is that you are also providing yourself with the answers that you need. Observe your metaphors, and make use of them.

If you spill blood, give blood.

If you want to jump in the water, jump in the water.

And if you are tired of walking on eggshells, get yourself a carton and tramp those suckers down.

Intervention #8: Choose a New Self-Image

The psychologist Dr. Joyce Brothers wrote: "An individual's self-concept is the core of his personality. It affects every aspect of human behavior: the ability to learn, the capacity to grow and change. A strong, positive self-image is the best possible preparation for success in life."

How you see yourself is crucial to your success. If you see yourself as a gangster and not to be messed with, you are headed toward injury, death, or prison. If you see yourself as a nice guy who never gets angry, you are going to caretake others. You'll be a doormat and take passive-aggressive potshots at the people around you - lying, sarcasm, forgetting to help them when you said you would, forgetting to return their phone calls, gossiping about them to others.

And yet, you are not a fixed personality. You *can* change. But, how?

Jim was a plumber. That's what he knew. It's what he did. That is, until the day he had an accident on the job and messed up his back. The State paid for him to go to vocational school, and he learned computer programming. Was he only a plumber? No. He had a completely untapped set of skills he knew nothing about.

You can be whatever you like. All you need to do is change how you see yourself and then declare the new you to the world.

> You can be whatever you like. All you need to do is change how you see yourself and then declare the new you to the world.

By now you are familiar with one of my favorite pet statements: "You are who you say you are." If you say you are a father, well, you are - though you have to determine specifically what kind of a father you are, and then you have to go out and *be* it; for example, wear "fatherly" clothes, talk in a fatherly manner, and so on.

Our negative patterns are kept in place by our self-talk, which is in actuality indicative of our self-definition. Whether I realize it or not, I define myself in terms of a broad category or archetype, be it "victim," "loser," "risk-taker," or "good ole boy."

Let me give you an example. A recent client, Henrietta, is oppositional, anti-authority, and self-pitying. Those are her three hallmark negative patterns. But if you were to sum this up as an archetype, you'd probably say that her self-definition is "Rebel." Now, she must determine for herself, "Do I want to remain a Rebel? Or would I prefer to veer off into another, more productive, more satisfying, less punitive self-image? Perhaps Artist, Visionary, Mother, or Teacher?"

> You are who you say you are

The universe, God, the Force - whatever you want to call it - is listening. If you say you are noble, the universe will listen to you. If you say you are caring, the universe will hear your words. In more down-to-earth terms, *you* are listening to *you*. And what you tell yourself greatly influences your actions. You are constantly giving yourself messages through your words, actions, and self-talk. "I'm a bad muthafucka," "I'm a funny guy," "I'm a scaredy cat," "I'm an emotional cripple," "I'm a hopeless romantic."

Billy was a strip club DJ with a soul patch under his lip. He wore dark clothing day and night. Everything about him was wild, reckless, and ego-based. His persona was out of balance. We worked on creating a new self-image for Billy. In every sinner there is a saint, and with that in mind we asked Billy to dress in white, to be silent rather than hyper-verbal, and to see himself as a father to his children rather than a partying dude.

As of the date of this writing, Billy is a success story. He has his struggles, but has largely turned his life around. He is a good father to his children, and gives his wisdom and experience to those in need. It all began with his telling himself and the world, "I'm a dad," and then following this new self-programming with deliberate actions to reinforce the message.

One of the inmates I counseled, McQueen, was a former heavyweight boxer of Caribbean descent who killed his mother's boyfriend in an argument over what they were going to eat for dinner. McQueen had a long psychiatric history prior to his heavyweight fighting career. He was diagnosed, at the time of his arrest, with Major Depressive Disorder with Psychotic Features.

According to reports, his father was depressed, and also had a history of violence. The father beat 4-year-old McQueen, putting him in the hospital while his mother was in a detox program. McQueen was removed from his parents' care and placed in a series of foster homes. In his teens, he was taught to box, which was a great outlet for an enraged kid. He became adept and won the Golden Gloves in his hometown.

McQueen's negative patterns, by his own admission, were excessive anger and impulsivity - a dangerous combination for a trained, violent man. How would you have worked with him? What would you have told him? To stop being violent? That wouldn't fly. His impulses got the better of him every time, and he acted out. Would you warn him of the consequences of his actions? Hell, he's sitting in prison for life. He knows where such actions will lead him. There's not that much more society can do to punish him.

McQueen repeats over and over again, "I can't help myself." He knows only violence as a solution to his problems, though he also repeats over and over again that he does not want to be angry or violent anymore *unless absolutely necessary.*

Notice that he's given himself an out. "I won't be violent - unless I have to." His belief system remains unchanged: "Violence is sometimes necessary." His self-image remains rooted: "I am mean and tough, and people better watch out for me." It would be impossible to help him shift his negative patterns unless and until he could change his self-image. But how to change his self-image?

I encouraged McQueen to see himself as a warrior, and not a thug. A warrior fights only when necessary and when he does so, it's to protect others. I asked McQueen to see himself as a *protector* rather than an attacker. But this meant that McQueen needed a community to protect. Well, we had one on the yard - the weak and defenseless. Did McQueen have to shed blood to protect them? Not really. He had a fearsome reputation in prison. Just a word of warning from him could keep others away.

McQueen struggled, but became less violent. He tried his best to take on the new role and, interestingly, he always sat near me during group. Though he never said it, I believe that McQueen wanted to be there to protect me, should trouble break out in the room.

What's your self-image? Who are you? How do you see yourself? More importantly, who would you *like* to be? Take a moment now to look over the list of positive archetypes below and find one or two that inspire you. Write a paragraph on the archetypes you choose.

In your paragraph, describe how you are already like this archetype. How might you increase the good qualities it represents? Or perhaps you've chosen an archetype that isn't much like the current you at all, but is someone you want to be in the future. Good! Write about what steps you'll take to get there. For instance, if you want to be a "Pioneer," what will you discover? What will you need in order to be a pioneer?

Fearlessness? A "can do" attitude? Funding? A degree?
A collaborator?

Please review the list below and circle all that apply
to you.

1. Apprentice
2. Artist
3. Athlete
4. Builder
5. Chef
6. Clown
7. Counselor
8. Defender
9. Detective
10. Engineer
11. Explorer
12. Father
13. Friend
14. Gambler
15. Godmother/Godfather
16. Healer
17. Hero
18. Journalist
19. King
20. Knight
21. Leader

22. Lover

23. Magician

24. Mediator

25. Mentor

26. Monk/Nun

27. Mother

28. Mystic

29. Nonconformist

30. Nurse

31. Philanthropist

32. Poet

33. Priest/Priestess/Minister/Rabbi/Preacher

34. Prince

35. Princess

36. Queen

37. Samaritan

38. Scientist

39. Seeker

40. Servant

41. Soldier

42. Speaker

43. Storyteller

44. Student

45. Teacher

46. Traveler

47. Warrior
48. Wise Man/Wise Woman
49. Wizard/Shaman
50. Writer

We are visual creatures. We hold images in our mind. That includes images of ourselves. These images become expectations and result in becoming what we create. Always, always, always, we need to keep our focus on what we do want, on who we want to become, rather than on what we don't like or don't want.

Intervention #9: Keep a Pattern Journal

This exercise is designed to help you stay vigilant about your patterns. When you're ready, go ahead and circle the negative patterns listed in Chapter 3 that best describe you. Choose one and write about it in a journal, asking yourself the following questions:

- When did I recently engage in that pattern?
- What triggered it?
- What causes me to engage in it?
- Where does it come from?

Here's Alan writing about his pattern of excessive anger:

When did I recently engage in that pattern?
A few days ago, I got very angry at my girlfriend. She kept telling me to check the air in the tires of my car, and I kept telling her I had already done it. I know she worries a lot 'cause I've had two accidents in the last three years. Besides, she worries a lot about everything.

What triggered it?
So she kept nagging me, and finally I yelled at her, "Stop it already, leave me alone!" I slammed the bedroom door, and stormed out of the apartment for an hour or two.

What causes me to engage in it?
Usually when I feel like people are bugging me, or nagging me, getting on my case, telling me what to do. I think that's it.

Where does it come from?

My dad used to always tell me what to do, and my mom was a constant nag. So I guess I've never liked it, and I never will.

Alan has had a lifelong pattern of feeling controlled. He has been passive, and not willing or able to assertively speak his truth to others, as in, "Honey, you already asked me to check the tires. I'll do it." Instead, he fumes and broods and explodes. His passivity and excess anger patterns are linked together. In fairness to his girlfriend, Alan may also be lazy, a procrastinator, incompetent, and/or careless (he has, after all, had several accidents). Alan ought to address these patterns as well, don't you think?

You may want to write about a recent event. Set down what happened, and how you felt about it.

When did I recently engage in that pattern?

What triggered it?

What causes me to engage in it?

Where does it come from?

Using interventions is the key to popping your patterns and changing your life! Start with the ones that interest or inspire you the most. It won't be long before you are feeling the positive effects of commitment to yourself and your growth.

Afterword

I hope this book has been of some help to you. I suggest you do the exercises, and, at the very least, learn to recognize your negative patterns of thought, emotion, and behavior. Do your best to diminish them, if only a little bit, and if only now and then.

Your life is a creation of your own choosing. If you were not aware that you had patterns, you are now! If you didn't know where they came from, you now know, or you're on the road to discovering their roots. You are on the way to having a great life, filled with love, joy, and serenity. It will take some time, but you'll get there. I did. You can, too. Be relentless. Practice rigorous honesty with yourself. Give your word and stick to it - no defeat, no surrender!

A bit of rigorous honesty on my part: I didn't know how to end this book. I thought and thought until it occurred to me, "A Brooklyn story - of course!" So here it is a Brooklyn story, sort of.

I was working at the maximum security facility in California, after having finally graduated school with my doctorate degree. I'd just received my license to practice psychology, and my brother, Brian, flew in from Seattle to help me celebrate at a backyard party hosted by a friend. Brian graciously made the toast, which went something like this: "My brother Seth left Brooklyn a long time ago. He avoided the gangs, steered clear of major trouble, got out of the neighborhood, and went to college. Years later, he moved to California, got a master's degree in psychology, did social work, got a doctorate in psychology, passed his licensure test - and still ended up in prison!"

I've come a long way from my childhood in Canarsie, Brooklyn, a longer and more eventful journey than I could ever have imagined back then. I hope your journey, too, is long and fruitful. May God, the universe, the Force - or whatever you want to call it - be with you.

I've popped many of my patterns along the way, an accomplishment of which I'm quite proud. I did it and so can you. Good luck with popping yours - the sky blue, pale violet, lemon yellow, snow white, mint green, cherry red, and chocolate brown.

Go, man, go!

Made in the USA
San Bernardino, CA
16 January 2016